Do More Than
Try -- Triumph !!

Talt O. Forrer

The Magnificent
MOTIVATORS!

The Magnificent Motivators

Royal Cassettes • Books • Speeches, Inc.
600 West Foothill Boulevard
Glendora, California 91740

First Edition

Library of Congress Cataloging in Publication Data in Progress

ISBN 0-934344-12-4

Printed in the United States of America

BEN FRANKLIN: MY LOVE!

by Dottie Walters, C.S.P.

They laughed and derided,
"Go fly a kite, Ben!"
But Ben just kept smiling.
A wise man. Ye ken?

He reached to the lightning
And tamed that wild beast.
He charted the oceans!
Ben's thoughts are like yeast,

Wherever he traveled
Minds Western or East.
Inquiring and learning
Exchanging a feast . . .

Of new ways to do things
With freedom and song!
I long for this friendship
I yearn to belong,

To Ben's merry comp'ny.
When my life is frightful,
Then I read his stories
His spirit delightful!

He sends hopes like kites up
"With teamwork, we CAN!
There's naught who can stop us . . .
COME, HERE IS A PLAN!"

Ben opens the floodgates
Of Genius for me,
Inventor, and statesman
With bright strategy.

His favorite expression
Of all I have read
"NOW, LET'S DO THE BUSINESS!
Come! Just use your head!"

(Adored by the ladies?
They loved him! Their "Sun!"
Now, need I inform you,
This lady is one?)

iv

DEDICATED TO AMERICA'S
FIRST MAGNIFICENT MOTIVATOR

Benjamin Franklin, 1704-1790, U.S.A.

Visionary. Patriot. Scientist. Engineer. Discoverer. Humorist. Author. Publisher. Enthusiast. Benefactor. Optometrist. Musician. Song Writer. Inventor. Health Advocate. Mariner. Dreamer. Weatherman. Athlete. Civic Organizer. Librarian. Educator. Naturalist. Farmer. Economist. Industrialist. Banker. Agriculturalist. Postmaster General. Inspirationalist. Diplomat. Strategist. Statesman. Editor. Newspaperman. Cartoonist. Advertising Genius. Manager. Botanist. Organizer. Humanist. Essayist. Poet. Internationalist. Printer. Business Executive. Promoter. Salesman. Abolitionist. Human Rights Advocate. Lover of People, Everywhere!

DOTTIE WALTERS

Dottie Walters' mother almost lost her at the seaside one day when the little girl disappeared from sight. After lifeguards, police and friends had searched for an hour, she was discovered sitting up on the boardwalk. In front of the five-year-old was a stack of pennies and a large quantity of "sand dollar" seashells.

"Why are you mad, Mommie?" Dottie beamed with joy. "I am so happy to be giving these people dollars for pennies!"

Dottie sold bouquets of wild flowers during the depression, had a doughnut route, organized a baby sitting service, ran ads and hired other teenagers, was advertising manager for her high school newspaper, then went to work, on the day after graduation, at the Los Angeles *Classified Department. When the recession hit her family, she bought space from a small weekly newspaper in Baldwin Park, California and walked to sell ads, pushing her two little children in a rickety old stroller. When the wheel kept falling off, Dottie gave it a whack with her shoe. But she never gave up. Local merchants knew her as a promise keeper who had fresh ideas for advertising copy. She finally earned enough to buy a Model A Ford. (A chunker, not an antique.)*

She began a newcomer welcoming service . . . used public speaking to promote her business: expanded it until she had the largest such service in the Western United States; wrote the first book on sales for women, the pioneer Never Underestimate the Selling Power of a Woman;*created cassette albums; has spoken all over the world; began a publishing company; organized a speakers booking agency and publishes and edits the largest newsletter for professional speakers in the world,* Sharing Ideas for Professional Speakers.

Dottie has spoken all over the United States, Asia, Canada, England and other foreign countries. Dottie and Bob Walters are parents of three fine children: an attorney, a teacher and a graphics art expert who leads the top Gymnastic Vaulting Team in the world— National Champions. The Walters have four grandchildren. Dottie is President of four corporations, and serves on the Board of Directors of other companies and organizations. Friends think of her as an inspiration, a mentor, a dynamic worker, poet and as Dottie often says herself, the most important, "an inspiration."

PROLOGUE
by Dottie Walters, C.S.P., Publisher
Certified Speaking Professional, National Speakers Association

"The art of speaking is an enchantment of the soul."
—Plato

Recently I spent a fascinating hour at a speakers banquet with Paul Green, an Industrial Organizational Psychologist from Memphis, Tennessee. Paul tests industrial job applicants. "Can you test for creativity or talent?" I asked him.

He replied, "Talent and creativity can be measured to some extent . . . but the most interesting thing is not if a person can achieve, but what causes a person to achieve! Skills can lie dormant until something triggers them."

"You mean hunger, fire, or even poverty?"

"Yes," Paul explained. "As the story goes, none of us knows we can climb a tree until the bear chases us!"

The Motivators

Often the trigger is the touch of a motivator. If you ask people of achievement what set them off, they invariably tell you, "I heard a great speech," "I saw a movie," or "I read a book." Often people will say, "I was inspired by my parents or teacher."

Paul Green's explanation reminded me of the story of the *Bridge on the River Kwai*. The ranking British officer is tortured. When at last he is released, his men fall in behind him, their spirits all spit and polish even though their bodies are covered in rags. They whistle as they march by quick step. He had motivated them to reach up to their higher potential.

Caesar's men called after him, "There goes Caesar, he is never discouraged!" Of course Caesar must have been handed problem after problem. But he stood up and showed a courageous attitude to his men. The famous painting of George Washington crossing the Delaware always reminds me of the "one to look up to" motivator. There was ice in the river, the boat was tippy, but Washington stood up so his men could *see him*.

The founder of modern nursing, Florence Nightingale, found men in the dirty Crimean hospitals with their faces turned to the wall. All hope gone. She cleaned them up, fed them, lighted their spirits, and healed them. They called her "The lady with the lamp." It was the spirits of the men she lighted with her motivational touch.

We all need motivators in our lives. They are magnificient. I love to read stories of people of achievement. This book is full of such inspiring material. Each chapter was written by authors who tell us, "Take heart," "Try again," "Go another way."

The Bible's Saint Paul told the early Christians, "PRESS FORWARD TO YOUR HIGHER POTENTIAL." Not relax, not lounge. Not tomorrow. NOW. What power Paul gave us in those motivational words PRESS FORWARD! The iron will of one brave heart can make a thousand quail, and rally gaints who have fled the battle of life.

Ben Franklin was motivated by Plato's words. Thomas Paine was motivated by Ben Franklin's words. When Thomas Edison was a young boy, failing in school, he was motivated by Tom Paine's *Age of Reason*. Tom Paine's words so motivated Edison he wrote, "They electrified me. Set me on fire. I was never the same again."

Motivation is a fire which burns down through the ages. It is a match which sets our lives aglow. We catch fire when we capture the vision the motivator gives us. Motivators generate dreams.

Who Are You?

Motivators are mirror holders. Through them, we can see ourselves as we could be. How do you see yourself? Are you a truck? A tractor, strong and sure? An airplane? If you were a machine, what would you be?

My own image is of the huge Star Ship, *Enterprise* from *Star Trek*. There are tiers of decks, lights ablaze, motors humming, crews working. Then sometimes I am hit by storms. The ship tilts. I am off balance, attacked, knocked to my knees, attacked, depressed. My lights are down. But then a great motivational thought comes my way. Possibly from the radio, or a book. Or I listen to a cassette in my car, or hear a speaker.

The motivational thought holds up to my inner eyes the image of the ship running, smoothly. I can see what can be.

Then the "Captain Kirk" of my mind gets up, takes to the bridge and grabs the helm. The captain decides how to solve the problems. Makes a plan. Organizes the crew. Uses the facilities at hand. Figures new ways to do the tasks that must be done, then gives the orders. The captain inspires confidence. Pulls the Star Ship back on course. The flight plan is set for unlimited possibilities.

I am the captain of my ship, as you are of yours.

Motivation is like a match which sets our lives alight. We catch fire when we capture the vision the motivator gives us. Before you step into this wonderful Anthology of Motivators, stop and think a moment. Who was the great voice, the towering figure in your life? Each motivator saw visions, dreamed dreams, looked ahead, pressed forward! Held up the mirror for you.

Trust Yourself

Who is following the path you are making? We have a responsibility to help those coming along behind us. Stand up! Not only for your own sake, but because others are watching you. You are precious. You have the ability. "Trust yourself. Every heart vibrates to that iron string." I learned the truth of that lesson from my own Magnificient Motivator, Ralph Waldo Emerson.

Be a Magnificient Motivator! Napoleon said, "There

is a baton of a general hidden in the knapsack of every foot soldier." The motivators in your life flash-fired the talent which God has already given you. Your job is to light the fires of those who watch you. When you strike the match with your own words and actions, through gifted eyes they see the possibility of their higher selves flamed with spirit and inspiration.

> "How the heart listened while the pleading speaker spoke
> While on the enlightened mind, with winning art
> The gentle reason so persuasive stole
> That the charmed hearer thought it was his own.
>
> —**Thompson**

The great deeds, ideas, actions, words *are your own.* You are the Captain of your life. Catch fire from the MAGNIFICIENT MOTIVATORS in this great book. TURN THE PAGE! WE ARE WAITING FOR YOU!

TROPOPAUSE
by Dottie Walters, C.S.P.

When jagged lightnings flash our plane
Wild winds and storms abound
We're knocked, then buffeted and hit
From take-off on the ground.

Our motors roar. We leap aloft
We break dark clouds. We soar!
Bright stars await us, always there.
The Captain smiles once more.

For here the quiet place is found
All turbulence below.
The pilots call it TROPOPAUSE
Where power thoughts fast flow.

When trouble hits your life force, stop.
Come! Switch your motor on.
Now set our ATTITUDE aloft
Soon turbulence is gone.

Just mark your flight path by the stars
Above life's troublesphere
Your TROPOPAUSE is waiting, friend.
Hope signals GO. ALL CLEAR!

(**Tropopause:** Calm region at top of the
troposphere, 7 to 10 miles above earth.
Portion in which clouds disappear and
storms are still. —*Webster.*)

BILL GOVE, C.P.A.E.
1A Atrium Circle
Atlantis, FL 33462
(602) 964-5225

Bill Gove, C.P.A.E.

Bill Gove, C.P.A.E., spent most of his business life at the 3M Company. He has spoken for thousands of companies all over the world in his 35 years on the platform. He is mentor to many speakers, helping them in their careers. Bill was the first President of the National Speakers Association. In 1980 he received the coveted Cavett Award from N.S.A. as "Member of the Year." Ty Boyd, also an N.S.A. past President and Cavett Award recipient, said, "If I had my wish, I would ask to be as good on the platform as Bill Gove!"

Bill holds his famous "Weekend Seminars" for aspiring speakers at his Florida headquarters, 1A Atrium Circle, Atlantis, Florida 33462, (305) 964-5225.

INTRODUCTION

A LOVE STORY . . .

by Bill Gove, C.P.A.E.

In 1930 I started selling house to house. In those days you didn't put your foot in the door; you put your head in! Then, if the housewife closed the door, you could keep on talking.

It was then that I met my first great Motivator, an energetic little guy named Cy Marcotte. We would all meet at 7:30 a.m. (might be the reason that I still feel guilty when I stay in bed later than that) and start the day by marching around the conference table singing, "Rise, Ye Men of Hoover!" Then Cy would go into his number. "Did the Wright Brothers quit?" he would ask. "NO!" we would cry out.

"How about Irving Loser? Did he quit?" asked Cy. At this point someone in the audience was cued to yell, *"I never heard of Irving Loser!"* Then Cy would hit us with his favorite line. *"That's because Irving Loser quit! That's why no one ever did hear of him, or ever will hear of him."*

Zillions of words have been written about Motivation, with most of the writers agreeing that you can't motivate anyone. All you can do is to create the environment in which the person motivates *himself.*

This great book then, is devoted to that rare breed of persons who has the unique talent for reminding all of us that the true joy in life comes from being as much as we can be.

If you agree that true love is a commitment *to* and and appreciation *of* another's true potential, then this book is a love story and all the great Speaker/Authors are lovers! Publisher Dottie Walters has done it again. Of course this will come as no great surprise to those of us who know her, because the lovely lady is the consummate Motivator herself. One can't be in her presence very long without wanting to remake the world.

Please don't try to read this book of love stories in one sitting. Keep it by your bedside. Digest its precious contents one bite at a time. Savor it. Remember it.

Enjoy!

As the Ancient Scot called out to friends as they left after a good visit, "Think of me. Dream of me!"

NORMAN K. REBIN, C.P.A.E.
P.O. Box 1240
Almonte, Ontario
Canada K0A 1A0
(613) 256-1080

Norman K. Rebin, B.A., MS.Sc., CSP, C.P.A.E.

For Norm Rebin, motivating others to reach beyond their present horizons is a cause—because, in himself, and in those who have worked with him, he has seen the results. His problem-solving, and people-involving approach skyrocketed his career through adult education directorship and diplomatic service abroad.

Achieving performance acclaim as he went, he discovered he still had extra physical, mental, emotional and psychic energy to expand his farming and his real estate developments; championing "avant garde" techniques in the former and cherishing heritage in the latter.

Dipping deeper into his well of untapped personal power, he then carried, through writing (a cousin of Tolstoy, he restricts his writing to children's books and management treatises), and speaking, this unique blend of philosophy coupled with his pragmatic "on-the-line" business experience and his ability to catalyze groups of various backgrounds and purposes, to clients on four continents. His skill and his style have made him a highly sought after speaker and executive consultant.

Through speeches tailored to each audience, and through practical examples relating to each audience member, Norm Rebin is able to teach individuals and groups to trust themselves and to try themselves . . . and, therein lies motivation.

FOREWORD
by Norman K. Rebin

Sophocles stated that "Heaven never helps the man who will not act." Doukhobors, a unique world sect, of which I am one, believe that we all "act out" our own heaven and our own hell . . . *here* on earth! To know whether a "heavenly" or a "hellish" fate will be your destiny, is not a question for God but a question for *you*.

Why am I what I am and what *motivates* me to "act" that way? Ask yourself that question as have the authors in this book. Discover why there is so little "chance" to life, only a series of contrived coincidences . . . contrived by your spirit, contrived by your common sense, contrived by your soul. What happens to us? Why do we win or lose? What can we expect? We become what we *are* and what we *do*. Life's real rewards, I am convinced, accrue only to those of dauntless spirit, directed common sense, and serenity of soul. Those who are motivated to achieve that blend will savor life's magnificience.

I look at fate, therefore, as the culmination of each person's attitude, aptitude, and action. Those who are serene of soul, at peace with themselves, liking and respecting what and who they are, will carry the most positive *attitudes*. Those who are dauntless of spirit, unfazed by change, undefeated by adversity, will "corral" the most positive *aptitudes*. Those who direct their common sense, not waiting for fate, but *creating* their fate, will command the most positive *action*. These qualities are "ingrained" in magnificent motivators! To them belong the just desserts of life for they truly "earn" while others "yearn." No easy formula for success tantalized them. No "hype" about being "superhuman" anaesthetizes them. They are a special breed . . . men and women of will, and of the wisdom to direct that will. Some are unsung heroes while others enjoy incredible stardom and superlative followings. Yet, they all subscribe to Oliver Wendell Holmes' adage that "the great thing in this world is not so much where we are, but in what direction we are moving."

I suspect that, like us, the magnificent motivators in this book have in their lives suffered occasional defeat and perhaps even dejection. They would be less able if they hadn't. For we in Canada, believe that the roughest seas hone the most skillful skippers. Although their exact position may have been tenuous, their direction was never in doubt.

I suspect that, like us, all the magnificent motivators in this book have tasted the pangs of occasional loneliness and rejection, too. Yet I suggest that they knew, as our ancestral friend Christian Bovee knew, that "active natures are rarely melancholy . . . and activity and sadness are incompatible!" So I presume these heroes and heroines just "drove on" despite the bruises on their souls or on their

HIGH FLIGHT
by John Gillespie Magee, Jr.

*This poem was written by an American volunteer in the Royal Canadian
Air Force who was killed in action December 11, 1941, at age 19.*

Oh, I have slipped the surly bonds of earth
And danced the skies on laughter-silvered wings;
Sunward I've climbed, and joined the tumbling mirth
Of sun-split clouds—and done a hundred things
You have not dreamed of—wheeled and soared and swung
High in the sunlit silence. Hov'ring there,
I've chased the shouting wind along, and flung
My eager craft through footless halls of air.
Up, up the long, delirious, burning blue
I've topped the windswept heights with easy grace
Where never lark, or even eagle flew.
And, while with silent, lifting mind I've trod
The high untrespassed sanctity of space,
Put out my hand, and touched the face of
God.

This poem was first published February 8, 1942 in the New York Herald Tribune

Contents

WILLIAM G. GRONINGER
Personal Development Institute
7718 Las Lilas
Citrus Heights, CA 95610
(916) 722-2244

William G. Groninger

Bill Groninger is the founder of Personal Development Institute and has been described as "having the rare commodities of sensitivity, honesty and self-assuredness that make him a great team asset and a unique person." He has successfully grasped a number of great challenges, both in and out of the military. Retired with the rank of Lieutenant Colonel, Bill has completed 20 years as an Air Force officer, including duties as a missile launch officer, navigator and pilot. He has flown 100 missions over North Vietnam, been an instructor in the supersonic T-38 trainer, a deputy commander of a missile site and the Chief of a Base Operations and Training Division. He also has the distinction of being one of a handful of pilots to have regularly flown the SR-71, the world's fastest airplane, at speeds of Mach 3 plus and above 80,000 feet.

Bill has instructed throughout the West on teamwork, management and communications with seminars for policemen, nurses, teachers, federal employees, managers, supervisors and others. He has addressed such organizations as Rockwell International, the Southland Corporation, Computer Science Corporation, Sierra Real Estate Trust, Washington Public Power Supply System, Army Corps of Engineers and many more. He is an excellent speaker and seminar leader. Follow his star!

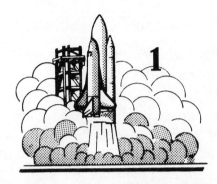

MACH 3 MOTIVATION HIGH FLIGHT
by *William G. Groninger*

"Oh, I have slipped the surly bonds of earth
And danced the skies on laughter-silvered wings . . ."

—John Gillespie Magee, Jr.

There we were, my navigator, Chuck Sober and I, flying in the SR-71 at three times the speed of sound, faster than 2100 m.p.h. and at approximately 80,000 feet. Nothing below us but hundreds of miles of ocean, a small island in the Pacific behind us and a tanker full of fuel ahead of us and waiting! We were approaching that awesome 400-mile stretch where, if one of our two engines failed or malfunctioned, we would not have enough fuel to travel on a single engine to the island behind us or to the tanker in front of us. As we entered the leg, just 12 minutes to the end, I could feel Chuck, in the cockpit behind me, shifting his weight into another position in an attempt to settle his uneasy feelings. I knew that's what he was doing, so was I. Eleven minutes left. Ten minutes, now. Nine, eight . . . the right engine let go. I knew it was the right engine because my head slammed off the left side of the cockpit. We were in trouble!

Motivation at three times the speed of sound, or is it three times the speed of sound motivation? That "word" creeps into our conversations at least once every day and what does it mean? What goes on inside that magnificent head of yours when someone mentions the word "motivation"? Do you see pictures? Do you hear sounds? Do you have feelings? What in the world does the word mean? Let's examine a little closer.

As I look at the word "motivation," I recognize that billions of dollars will be spent this year on motivational material. Businesses will spend, the government will spend, individuals will spend; buying a package, hiring a person, or seeking something that will inspire move-ment. If we could only know what it is that motivates each and every person, imagine the huge impact we could have in changing lives, changing the world! Just imagine what it would be like if you had the key to the lock! Just imagine!

But, you *do* have the key. You know what motivation is to you and I can give odds that it's the same for at least one other person. So let me share with you what inspires me to move into action, knowing at least one person who reads this will say, "Yes, that's right, that's me 100 percent." To you, my friend, my heart and mind are yours right now, we are a team. Ah, my secret.

Teamwork is my motivation. A team and its support systems are the keys to the successful encounters in my life. When I'm dragging and most discouraged, I feel alone. I've kept everyone away from me and I make it a self-fulfilling prophecy. But, when I'm up, I know my team is really working together, we are all supporting each other and we're winning! Are you a winner? Of course you are. Would you like to stay there? Of course you would. I'm going to.

Our whole world is a team and motivation can be nothing more than creating an environment where people can extend their limits, test themselves, have a chance to succeed beyond their expectations or fall short and still maintain their dignity. No one operates in a vacuum anymore. Competitors, from the distance runner to the boxer, operate as part of a team, a support system. Their motivation becomes the environment their team creates and the support system to which they become attached. Motivation comes from within, not from without! So, let me show you my team and how it worked for me. It's called Mach 3 Motivation.

Alone, Unarmed and Scared to Death

Some years ago, the Air Force made a film on reconnaissance crews and entitled the movie, "Alone, Unarmed and Unafraid." We in the business changed it to read "Alone, Unarmed and Scared to Death." Alone, unarmed and unafraid? Or scared to death? Which one is it? How do you decide at three times the speed of sound, Mach 3, nearly 2200 miles an hour or close to 35 miles a minute? How do you decide and how did we get there? Let me tell you how it began.

It all started with a team. That magnificently beautiful task of molding a team together. Through the agonies, the triumphs, the headaches and the growing pains of making a team. Supporting each other, comforting each other and making it work. And that, of course, is how we make it through the "tough ones," by creating win-win situations for all of us; by grasping hands with each other, and working not alone, but together.

My navigator and I were a team. We were like a marriage. We respected each other, supported each other, got angry with each other, laughed and played together. He was my partner, my Reconnaissance Systems Officer. Chuck was a big, gentle man, about 6'3" and 220 pounds, mild-mannered, dedicated, intelligent and truly a professional. We went everywhere together. We needed to be a team. At nearly 35 miles a minute, you don't deliberate long in making decisions. We had to know how each of us thought and felt and we needed to know all the meanings and implications of the words that we used in our communications. We were together all of the time. Our names (Groninger/Sober) appeared on everything. In fact, once when I went to the Lockheed representative's office, the secretary looked at me and asked, "Do you have a drinking problem?" I said, "Heavens no, I don't have a drinking problem. What in the world are you talking about?" She replied, "Well, I thought you must have a drinking problem because every time I see your name I see Sober after it."

We were always together and the job required both of us. I flew there and back; he did everything else. He was the information collector. He couldn't get there without me, and I couldn't work without him. The whole process of being a crew, of working together and training as a team was a tremendous support system. In your personal lives, do you have a support system like that; do you have the kind of support for Mach 3 flight?

Chuck and I were motivated to perform as a team because of the environment and because of our support systems. The environment required us to work very hard at nullifying any differences between us. To enjoy excellence and even survival, we had to be "in time," synchronized with each other. The desire to excel as partners was the guiding factor in our motivation to win and to reach "Mach Threedom." The environment created the need and we filled that need because we wanted to have the identity of that support system. And now that we had it and we were in the environment, how would we stay there? What would motivate us to remain in the alone, unarmed and scared to death business?

The Suit Up

It was 0030 hours by my clock. I wanted just ten more minutes sleep so I touched the snooze button that would wake me once again; but from lighter sleep. At 0040 I was up. We had a long mission today and I was rested and ready. We had done our flight planning and reviewed the computer navigational material the day before, so we were prepared. I'd meet Chuck in 30 minutes and we would drive to breakfast—steak and eggs—and then to our detachment for the pre-mission briefing which would include weather, intelligence and a precise review of the mission requirements. A brief physical examination and then we'd be ready to enter the next portion of our journey and meet with the next team, the folks who dressed us before we went out to play.

The Physiological Support Division (PSD) had the responsibility of dressing two grown men. It was their job to assist us in putting on our pressure suits and to make absolutely certain, 100 percent sure that, if the suits were needed in a life and death situation, they would work. They, too, operated in pairs as a team. Each of us now had a highly trained, extremely competent and motivated team giving us all of their attention.

The proper clothing is essential for high altitude flight. We wore a full pressure suit, which is basically the same suit the astronauts wear. Anytime you go above approximately 60,000 feet, your blood boils if you are exposed to the atmosphere. That doesn't mean it boils because of temperature. In fact, it comes out of the body because of a lack of pressure. In that environment, the only way to sustain life is to maintain positive pressure on the body by wrapping the pressure suit around it. The suit acts as a cacoon, provides pressure on the body so that the 100 percent oxygen supplied in the helmet can be absorbed at the cellular level. So believe me, our concern over whether or not it was going to work was real.

Slipping into the suit from the back, we put our legs in one at a time. They pulled the suit up to our knees, then inserted our arms one at a time; now a duck of the head, a slight push and the head popped through the neck ring, a zip up the back and the suit was on. Helmet, boots and gloves completed the wardrobe. Our survival could depend upon the clothes we were wearing and our lives were in the hands of the two people who were standing beside us now as they strapped on our last piece of equipment, our spurs (fastened to steel cables at the base of each ejection seat and used to restrain our feet during the ejection sequence). We trusted our lives to these teammates. Can you do that?

Is there suit-up motivation on your team? The team members who were the PSD technicians and suited us for flight were also motivated by their team environment. The sense of teamwork, the responsibility of protecting lives, the trust placed in them, the pride in being an integral part of a support system was their motivation and it came from within. The environment created the need, they supplied the work, and the team supplied the trust to feed the motivation. Is your team in an environment that creates enough motivation for you to trust your life to them?

The team was expanding now and the need for motivation was also expanding. The larger the environment becomes, the greater the team requirement and the greater the need for support systems. Our systems were most certainly growing and the need for teamwork and motivation was becoming even more critical.

After our PSD technicians had connected us to the airplane systems (oxygen, vent, parachute and ejection seat) and our ground crew added the final touches to their creation, we were ready to accelerate our huge engines, each exceeding the thrust of the Queen Mary, and begin taxiing for takeoff.

Takeoff—Refueling

The time had passed quickly. We were in the last 30 minutes prior to our 0400 takeoff time. It was still very dark. Chuck commented, "Not many stars tonight." I responded, "Charlie"; (meaning, that's correct). Our ground crew had completed their hours of painstaking labor to ready the aircraft for flight. All of the required equipment was on board, serviced and prepped for the tedious tasks ahead. Nearly fifty people stood to the sides of the airplane, waiting now, fingers crossed, feeling a sense of commitment, common purpose and pride in themselves and trust in their teammates. I could see the commitment in their faces and feel their support. They wanted us to be safe and sound.

Our checks were complete, the engines were running, each start assisted by two Buick Wildcat engines. The flight controls were checked, the crew chief had closed each canopy and hurried to the front of the airplane. He motioned to us to begin moving; we did. He saluted and I returned it. The others acknowledged with a thumbs-up, meaning OK. It wouldn't be long now, just a few more checks.

Upon reaching the runway and prior to taxiing into takeoff position, we finished our final checks. I paused a moment and reflected upon how large a team we had become. The number of people who actively contributed to Chuck and me being there had grown in size far beyond those I could see, several hundred now. The thread that held us all together was the commitment to a common purpose. The environment demanded motivated people, the purpose provided the bond; we were the team!

It's now 0355 and the tower advised us to take the active runway and shortly thereafter authorized takeoff. At 0400 sharp I began to move both of the throttles in my left hand, the engines began their rhythmic dance to reach full afterburner power. A release of the brakes and we're rolling, slowly at first and then faster, faster, faster. A slight tug on the stick and the nose is in the air. We're off, we're flying. The ground crew usually watched until we were out of sight. The brilliant blue of the afterburners would glow until extinguished at about 20,000 feet and they would be watching intently until we were no longer visible. Now, the highly motivated team would have to wait.

The common purpose drew the team even closer together as they monitored us minute by minute. We were flying but in a sense, each one of them was also; for each had a seat on our shoulders and were our teammates and encouraged us with their trust and support. They waited for us to return, to be reunited and, once again, become a whole. They felt every bump and they saw every star we did. They sweat every drop from each pore that we did and they were just as exhausted as we upon our return. The excitement and renewed energy would again fill the air as our return time grew near.

Refueling—Motivation Resupply

One of our most sensitive areas was just ahead of us now. We were preparing for refueling, that delicate operation of bringing two airplanes together and keeping them physically connected for perhaps 30 minutes. This was our greatest test of teamwork because it required two teams, the tanker and us. Again, both teams had that central purpose and the underlying commitment to accomplish the mission. Our motivation here, too, resulted from the environment we had achieved, and we were ready to perform and excited about the challenge.

The tanker would always take off before us and check the weather in the refueling area. They would orbit in a designated track, at an appointed time and at a specific point in space. When we arrived, we would be separated by 2000 feet in altitude. Gradually we would close in and meet. Finding them had been complicated by bad weather, not to mention the darkness. However, Chuck was the best; he electronically found the tanker and directed me to within one mile of the "Christmas tree" looking KC-135. As I readied the aircraft for refueling and closed into the pre-contact position, I couldn't help thinking that I was very glad I could trust the guys in front of us. I knew them and respected their ability and I knew that, above all else, they were a highly trained, exceptionally capable and dedicated team. They were committed to accomplish the job, being motivated by pride in themselves and driven by our mutual purpose.

The clouds, the darkness and the lights of the tanker confused my senses so much that I developed vertigo. I wasn't certain if I was right-side-up or upside-down. Chuck kept talking to me and telling me we were "wings level." Had it not been for my partner, I would not have been able to safely continue the refueling. Finally, after what seemed like a lifetime, we had a pressure dis-connect from the tanker. We were full. The inside of my pressure suit was soaked with perspiration; I felt weak. The muscles in my arms and legs were tense, but I was proud. We had once again proved that our common purpose and the support of a team had motivated us all to new and exceptional heights. Our two teams had just been the strings and the bow of a Stradivarius. Magnificent!

Mach 3—Hi-Speed Motivation

We were alone now; it was up to us to complete the reconnaissance portion of our mission. Separated and clear of the tanker, we began our "dipsy doddle" maneuver, which was a climb of about 10,000 feet and then an accelerated descent. The maneuver rapidly propelled us through the sound barrier, which is an area of instability for an aircraft, and now permitted us to begin the accelerating, climbing profile that makes the SR-71 so unique. We were at Mach 2 now, above 60,000 feet and still accelerating and climbing; the airplane was working perfectly just like our ground crew said it would. We were approaching level off and three times the speed of sound. In another moment or two, I'd have the airplane configured for several long cruise legs.

Since the plane is such an extremely complicated piece of machinery, my task was one of fine turning this incredible black beauty. Each airplane had a personality of its own and this one was positive, strong, yet very sensitive and required a gentle touch. However, this baby had a reputation! Every once in awhile, and without a great deal of warning, one of the engines would cough, spit, sputter and sometimes quit. I didn't feel that it would happen today though, because this tough yet sensitive machine felt strong and hummed with perfection. All was well.

There was a moment now to just review the instruments, so I felt somewhat relaxed. However, I never really relaxed in the airplane because in an instant, the flash of an eye, a problem could develop that would make for a very short day. As the pace slowed slightly for me, and as frequently happens when there's time to think about things, I realized I had need for a restroom. Now, as you can imagine, I couldn't excuse myself, get up and use the facility. I can't stop the plane and get out, but I could use the relief device that I had put on before my pressure suit earlier in the morning. It was a difficult task, psychologically, to say the least, since I had to reprogram myself to feel that it was all right to relieve myself in my pants; what Mom had taught me not to do! In addition, it reminded me of an incident that had happened to a friend of mine on a six-hour mission in the U-2 aircraft, the forerunner to the SR-71.

My friend was concerned about the length of time he would have to stay in the pressure suit and after a long deliberation, he decided to wear his device for the very first time. Many of the crewmembers just couldn't use it, so they never wore it. However, for some, overwhelming discomfort had a way of changing one's mind; it had for him. But, no one told my buddy that the device was adjustable and, since it came in only one size, he had some difficulty. His suit-up, takeoff, climb and all else had been normal except . . . One hour after takeoff, he was back in the local area having declared an emergency with the Air Traffic Controllers.

The very word emergency, even spoken at a whisper, makes some uncomfortable because it generates a whole host of activity and excitement in preparation for a possible disaster. The airfield suddenly becomes an army of ants all after one piece of candy. The fire trucks and the crash crews, an ambulance and a Flight Surgeon, the Wing Commander, Chief of Base Operations, and everyone having anything to do with airfield operations, medical care and emergency rescue, race to their positions and attempt to discern the reason for the *EMERGENCY* and what the expected actions might be. Well, as you can imagine, when they learned what had generated the problem, it became very funny, except to my friend. He was extracted from the aircraft and rushed to the hospital for an *EMERGENCY* removal of the device.

Although this story ended well and rather humorously for my friend, he later had another emergency that did not. All of the same agencies responded, but this time it wasn't humorous and it did not end well. He died. Because they were part of a highly trained and exceptionally motivated team, they responded for the single purpose of support. The people were dedicated to a common purpose and their motivation was controlled by the environment. When an aircraft and an aircrew are in danger, they are ready to respond, to give of themselves to save a life. No one told them they had to perform the job of rescue, they chose it because they wanted to. The external requirements demanded motivation and the people summoned it from within because we were a team, and a mighty good one.

Our airplane was still working perfectly; we had finished our "take leg" and were heading toward that last refueling. We still had that ominous 400-mile stretch that had to be flown before feeling the comfort of closing in behind our second refueling tanker for the day. It had been a beautiful sunrise and, at present, there wasn't a cloud in the sky. Just a few more minutes and we'd begin that awesome stretch. We both shifted in our ejection seats, the airplane was precisely tuned, it purred with perfection. Chuck commented, "We're beginning the 400-mile leg now." I noted the time, 11 minutes, 10, 9, 8, and . . . The right engine inlet had decided to take a fit and spit the supersonic air out of the inlet. It acted like a compressor stall. But why now, damn it, why now? The engine did it again and again, three times our heads had bounced off the left side of the canopy. I quickly took manual control of the engine inlet, but we had lost speed and altitude and it was going to cost us a lot of fuel to get back on track. Chuck read me the emergency checklist and, as I completed the items, the problem seemed to clear itself, just as quickly and as mysteriously as it had attacked us. The engine seemed normal but our fuel wasn't; we had a problem.

Quick computations of the fuel remaining made it very clear that our worst fears had come true. We were critically short on fuel and the only way we'd make it was with help from our tanker in front of us. They received our message and volunteered what we needed, they turned to come and meet us. They would place themselves in a compromised position to support us. The environment demanded and they provided.

Touchdown

The happy ending is that our teammates came far enough toward us so that we could rendezvous and they would give us enough fuel to get home. Their willingness and motivation to "go the extra mile" put them in a compromised fuel condition as well. But they, too, made it home safely.

We all supported each other to the benefit of all. The airplane was home, we were home, the tanker and their crew were safe, and our ground crew had a job to do to find out what caused our problem and to ready the "bird" for the next flight. Our team was once again a whole and our environment would demand that we perform again and we were ready and motivated because we chose to perform. We controlled it inside of ourselves through pride and a dedication to a common purpose.

Have you looked inside yourself to see what causes you to move? What did you find? Are you waiting for magic or did you find your secrets? Create your environment, have others join you and build a common purpose. Make your own music, take your particular magic and build your own Mach 3 team. Suit up with the right clothes for your mission; come down from speed and altitude long enough to refuel. Have a team that will reach out and take a risk for you because you all need each other.

Be willing to dare, be willing to care; but most of all, be willing to be *you*. Test the air where never lark or eagle flew and trespass on the sanctity of space because you, too, can put out your hand and touch the face of **God!**

"Action may not always bring happiness, but there is no happiness without action."

—Disraeli

JACQUES WEISEL

Sales Motivation Consultant
Woodland Court, Suite 366
Coram, NY 11727
(516) 698-7760

Jacques Weisel

Jacques Weisel brings to the lecture podium a distinguished background of sales and motivational training.

As a highly skilled professional salesman he was the #1 producer for several international companies, which had a total of over 14,000 sales reps. Jacques now conducts sales training and motivational seminars all over the United States and is also a highly sought-after banquet speaker. He is a published author, writing a weekly column for several newspapers entitled Positive Living. *He also hosts his own TV show, which is now in its third year. It also is called* Positive Living.

Jacques is currently the President of the New York-Metro Chapter of the National Speakers Association. He is also a member of LINC and ASTD of Long Island. He is an adjunct teacher at C.W. Post College, and at the New York Institute of Technology, where he teaches Public Speaking; How to Close Sales; How to Develop a Positive Mental Attitude;and How to Increase Profit Thru Better Sales Management. Some of his many REPEAT clients include Century 21, Mary Kay Cosmetics, Sears, the Ford Motor Company, Home Improvement Council of New York, Life Underwriters Associations, AIKD, Chiropractic Associations, Amway, Singles Groups, PWP, schools and libraries.

HOW TO BECOME SELF—MOTIVATED FOR SUCCESS
by Jacques Weisel

"You cannot teach a man anything. You can only help him discover it within himself."

—Galileo

Over a century ago the great philosopher-humanist Henry David Thoreau wrote the following: "The mass of men lead lives of quiet desperation." Today, this can be paraphrased to read: "LOUD desperation, not by their words alone but by their deeds." Success and failure in life take up the same amount of time. If a person spends 40 hours per week on the job, and 20 more worrying about the bills, inflation, etc. . . . he is in reality spending 60 hours per week "on the job." Well, that's about how many hours per week your success-oriented person spends between working at it, and thinking and making it easier, better and more profitable. The difference lies in the attitudes (+ or -) brought into these hours.

If your personal success barometer has not yet reached the Altitude you expected in life, don't look to your Aptitude Level as your problem, since this represents only 15 percent of success in any endeavor. Look rather to your Attitude which is responsible for 85 percent of whatever levels of success and peace of mind you attain in life. Since Attitude is governed by personal *self-esteem,* it is to this most important subject that I wish to address myself.

Having lived my entire childhood with a very low self-esteem, I can fully appreciate its destructive power. Born in Belgium of the "wrong" religion, I was programmed for extermination by the Nazis at the age of eight. We ran from them and landed in Casablanca, Morocco, where we were put in a detention camp. I was not allowed to attend regular school, thereby losing three years of education. The country was invaded by the Americans in 1942; we were rescued and came to the States in 1943.

My already low self-esteem took a turn for the worse after landing here. Thanks to radio and newspaper advertising, I discovered I had bad breath, dandruff and body odor. I was also rated inferior by my peer group, since I did not speak English (at the time I only spoke three languages). That's when I took a class in Remedial English, remedial meaning "curative," as if I had a disease which could infect other kids. Actually it was the other way around, as I had become infected with a "Brooklyn" accent for which there is no known cure.

How good (or bad) do you feel about yourself? In other words, what is your Self-image? Did you hug yourself today? . . . Yup, I do mean yourself. Because if you don't psychologically hug yourself first, any other hugging you do will become meaningless. Here's what I mean. Grandparents with a low self-esteem beget parents with a low S.E., who beget children with a low S.E., who in turn beget grandchildren with a low S.E., and so on, etc. . . . get the message? In his classic work *Reality Therapy*, Dr. William Glasser says we all have the same two basic mental needs; the need to love and be loved, and to feel worthwhile to ourselves and to others. Our health and happiness depend on having huge doses of both needs on a regular basis.

On a scale of 0 to 100% where do you stand on the loved/loving meter? How about a measuring spoon on self-worth? Do you fill the spoon, or barely a drop? Life is really very simple. *You are what you think about all day long!* When you're ready to face reality, sit down and figure out what went on in your mind the past day. If you truly like what you see, keep thinking it. If you don't like it, change it! How? Well, a good start would be to follow Robert G. Ingersoll's advice. He said, "My creed is this: Happiness is the only good. The place to be happy is here. The time to be happy is now. The way to be happy is to make others so." I think his message speaks for itself.

Life is a funny thing; it gives us exactly what we order from it. Does this mean that we "order" poverty, sickness and general unhappiness in life? Very definitely YES, if our outside actions are not consistent with our personal, or internal beliefs. Let me explain. If you are not now following the code of ethics you were brought up with, you carry the great burden of GUILT on your psychological shoulders. This means you have not earned the right to enjoy life and the good things it has to offer. Therefore, you must pay the price with a low self-esteem. As a nation we have become so enthralled with the word STRESS we feel it is the *cause* of many of our problems. Not so. It is really the *effect* of our own self-imposed physical and mental limitations, triggered by how we approach the outside world we live in.

The simple fact is, you can't change *other* people. You can't even change situations at times. But you can change YOURSELF. Socrates said, "Know thyself" . . . perhaps he should have added . . . "Then change thyself." Find out WHO YOU ARE, WHAT YOU WANT, and *how to get it*. Develop a positive mental attitude, which means getting rid of outdated guilts. Set personal and financial goals, go after them *ethically,* since this is the only way you'll be able to enjoy the fruits of your labor. Psychologists tell us that we are so busy tripping over our OWN FEET we never get past the starting gate in the race of life . . . or as Pogo once said, "We have met the enemy and he is US." Become your best friend by respecting and liking yourself. Only then can you respect and like your fellow man.

Empedocles, the Greek philosopher (490-430 B.C.) said, "We would have inner peace, but will not look within." Systematic, in-depth, soul-searching will reveal to you that most of your present day thoughts come from the *outside* world. They can, therefore, be sent back to where they came from. Instead, develop and use your own "intuition," or *learning from within.*

When Michelangelo was asked how he came to sculpt the statue of David, here's what he said: "I took a block of granite, and I chipped away everything that was not David . . ." Learn to chip away whatever is not the *real* you, but has been piled on you by others, who were always trying to mold you into their *image!* Hey, I thought that was God's gig! How come so many people think they can improve on that? Michelangelo knew the formula, and brought *David* out of the granite. Not another Michelangelo.

Warning: The Surgeon General Has Determined that Apathy Is Dangerous To Your Health

Most people have an aim in life, but no ammunition. You're at a picnic and you spot a young man with an archery set, shooting arrows into tree trunks. Every time he hits a tree he goes over and paints a perfect bullseye around the arrow. Passersby who only see the results of his work think he is a great archer. You smile, knowing better of course. Or do you? . . .After all, isn't this basically the way you run your life? You end up somewhere, and then decide that's where you wanted to be all along. As a mature individual you've forgotten the most basic concept of living which is to plan ahead. You'll go over the day-by-day activities for a two-week vacation (perhaps 50 vacations in your lifetime) as if you were involved in a forcible overthrow of a hostile government. Yet your only *once-in-a-lifetime* journey is played through without too much rhyme or reason, usually with no plan beyond today and what it *may* bring. The Koran says, "If you don't know where you are going, any road will get you there."

It's a well-known psychological fact that man is a goal-striving mechanism. This means that whether he has goals or not *he will reach them.* My question is simply this. Would you rather reach goals which are yours, or someone else's? As a child we were given short-range goals to live by. "Eat your food," "Go to bed," "Don't step in the gutter," "Go to college," "Get married," etc. . . . all short-range and long-range plans that someone else wanted us to execute. It's no wonder that we got out of that habit as soon as we could . . . and usually end up by throwing out baby with the dirty water. Goals are not important to positive living. They are *crucial.* It is not a coincidence that the word goal begins with "go." Daily goals give you the best reason to get up and do. Weekly goals make the months fly, and monthly goals renew your enthusiasm for life twelve times per year. Annual goals can guarantee a lifetime of successful happenings, as you maintain full control of your personal destiny.

Just as the captain of a ship does not need to see his destination thousands of miles away to know he will reach it at a certain date and time, so can you plan your life according to your own timetable. Your goals must be realistic and reachable, so that you can reap the rewards of positive reinforcement at timed intervals, and thus have the confidence to know that you're on target for the big plan.

One last condition. You must feel *you deserve* to

reach your personal and financial targets, and only a *healthy self-esteem* can do that. As children we are all either the victims or beneficiaries of attitudes instilled in us by others. We are either cursed or blessed by our early conditioning . . . and we also know that the Bible says, "As a man thinketh in his heart so is he." This means that if we don't like some of our "programmed" thinking, we can change it by putting stronger and healthier thoughts into our minds.

We should, perhaps, heed the words of the Apostle Paul, "Forgetting those things which are behind and reaching forth unto those things which are before." Translated into modern-day English I think he was espousing the psychological concept of PMBO (Personal Management By Objectives). In other words, he told us to leave the past in the past, and to move decisively forward into the future. I think he would have agreed with Confucius (551-479 B.C.) who said: "A superior man is free from fear and anxieties."

One last good thought on goals by Henry David Thoreau: "The man who goes alone can start today. But he who travels with another must wait till that other is ready." Nuff said . . .

How to Add Spice to the Menu of Life!

For the success recipe of your life try this. Take a sprig of desire, mix it liberally with a sauce of willpower, add two spoonful of purpose, top it off with a dash of persistence. Shake well in the blender known as *life*, and drink slowly, as this magic elixir can propel you to any heights your mind can conceive.

My business card reads Motivator, Sales Trainer. People must often want to know how I motivate anyone into better performance. They all look for the *magic button* which will turn them into driving dynamos of success in their chosen field of endeavor, *immediately!* Where we are concerned, time is of lesser consequence, since it is mainly a state of mind. When we're enjoying life, we forget time . . . when we're unhappy we count every second as a personal affront against us. People who want to change their lives and become more positive tend to forget that it may have taken 20, 30, 40 years or more to reach their present level of negativism. It also did not manifest itself at the touch of a button. Fortunately, it does not require another bunch of years to turn us around. What is required is *consistency of purpose.*

An important addition to this concept is the theory of *affirmations.* Psychologists have found that daily affirmations of what you want to become "grease the path" for these self-help ideas. Visualizing yourself as you used to be, using old photographs, etc. . . . will reinforce your will to become thinner if that is your wish. Concentrating on a small goal such as a *daily victory* over gluttony rewards Self-Esteem. Continued rewards to our self-image makes it easier to change from what we are to what we want to become. And these concepts work on all habits we wish to change.

Herbert Otto, philosopher-writer said it this way: "We are all functioning at a small fraction of our capacity to live fully in its total meaning of loving, caring, creating and adventuring. Consequently, the *actualizing* of our potential can become the most exciting adventure of our lifetime." Right now, as the figures stand, only two people out of every hundred have mastered these concepts, and are busily enjoying the fruits of their labors. What I mean is, if you must work to survive, work in such a way that the rewards will be mostly *yours*. Not for some stranger (boss) who decided to work you for *his* gravy-train.

Persistence also means getting cooperation from others, such as friends and relatives. If they are against your ideas, don't discuss what you plan with them. Do your thing *secretly* if you must, and then share the *results* with others. Their negatives will have no effect on you then.

If, on the other hand they love you, they will support your ideas. Unfortunately, when it comes to solving our problems, one wit has said: "Eighty percent of the people you tell your problems to don't care, and the other 20 percent are glad you have them."

Also, if your fear of criticism is greater than your desire for positive change, you will fail. It's been well documented that the quality most prized by and exhibited by two of the giants of the past century was *persistence*. I'm referring to Henry Ford and Thomas Edison, creative genuises "san pareil" (i.e. without equal).

My faithful dictionary says on persistence: "continuing *especially* in the face of opposition; stubborn." Do not be afraid to be stubborn for what you believe in. It's a prized quality. Latest statistics show that almost 80 percent of all Americans are seeking self-fulfillment. Ralph Waldo Emerson said this of human behavior: "What you *are* screams so loud I can't hear what you *say*"!!! Be a model of your convictions!

How to Sell Yourself to $UCCE$$!

Selling yourself and your ideas to others is one of the most important needs man has. Some experts call this the "ability to communicate." All agree that it makes for happier, more positive living. My query today is; how would *you* like to learn the secret of selling yourself, and your ideas? After all, positive living dictates that you learn to handle one-to-one situations. And to do it in such a way that more people will want to do as you suggest.

First rule is, learn to deal with people on an *emotional level*. Numerous studies have shown that our buying habits follow a 90 to 10 formula. In other words our "thinking" brain is only 10 percent as large as our "feeling" brain. Speaking to people using *factual* information will not move them toward acceptance of your ideas. To *move* people, you must *motivate* . . . and you motivate by stirring emotions (e-motion = move). Unfortunately, many of us are literally shortsighted when it comes to other people. As a result, the way we see them is the way we end up treating them. As we end up treating them, they end up *becoming!* You have the power to change people by the way you see and treat them. Truly an *awesome responsibility*.

I teach the same concept in professional selling. Sales managers are, as a rule, notoriously undertrained for their positions. They usually treat their sales staff *as they are*. Thusly, they fail to get that extra mile out of them. There's a "baker's dozen" hidden inside every sales rep.

Yet the sales manager (or is it mangler?) only shoots for the usual dozen when getting sales goals, and misses.

My best philosophy on selling comes from the great German writer, Goethe, "If we take people as they are, we make them worse. If we treat them as if they *were* what they ought to be, we help them to become what they are capable of being."

A survey was done several years ago which analysed 100 self-made millionaires. Only one common denominator bound them together. These highly successful men and women could only see the *good* in others. They were people-builders, not critics. Speaking of critics, you'll never read about any of them in your history books. Simply because they do not help make history. Instead, they're usually on a lifelong "search and destroy" mission. Critics leave their victims worse off for having met them. As for constructive criticism, there's no such thing. The words belie the term. Critics could never understand what Harvey Firestone once said, "You get the best out of others when you give the best of yourself!"

Getting back to the art of selling yourself, here's rule No. 2. Do *not do* to others what you *would not* want done to you. Look at the world through their eyes, not yours. Say and do what will excite *them* and interest *them.* And for the *millionth* time, make them feel *important!* You can change *lives* by using these age-old concepts, and they cost you nothing. Human relations do not work . . . humane relations do. The difference in the words is an E, perhaps for extra Effort. You can acquire a Ph.D. (People-Handling Doctorate) overnight once you begin to use this non-magical formula. Test-try it for 30 days. If it doesn't get you the desired effect, you can always go back to being a miserable person to be around. Or, as the joke goes, you'll remain the type of person who brightens up a room . . . by leaving it!

A great majority of the people I do business with have not yet learned to let go of the *I* for the *you*. They seem to travel on their own *Ship of Fools,* going nowhere fast in the trip of life. They look for help in their relationships from the outside. They forget that the greatest helping hand they can find is attached to their own wrist.

Another quality you must cultivate is the art of being dependable. People will pay more, both in money and attention, to someone who exhibits depend-*ability,* than one who only shows ability. Ability in this world is rampant, *depend-*ability rare. So, become the rare person you were meant by your Creator to be.

**Positive Living Works

P - Prime reason for living is to help mankind to improve.

O - On hatred, it makes the holder of it sicker than the recipient.

S - Since we are our own worst enemy, we can also become our best friend.

I - Interesting women turn me on longer than beautiful ones.

T - The more you give of yourself, the more you have left over.

I - I can live with my faults more easily when I forgive the faults of others.

V - Valuing my privacy, I am also happy in the company of others.

E - Enthusiasm is the greatest force on earth. It's free, unpolluted and abundant.

L - Life is beautiful, people not always.

I - I am color-blind when it comes to people.

V - Vengeance erodes self-respect.

I - I love my work, therefore I work my love.

N - Non-resolved anger eats up the healthy body cells, turns them cancerous.

G - Greed is the result of an inferiority complex.

I challenge each and every one of you to a renewed dedication to the pursuit of excellence . . . I challenge you to surpass your previous best . . . I challenge you to reach new heights in positive living. Realize your full potential . . . dedicate yourself to become the person you once thought you could be . . . Let your spirit soar with the eagles, and your mind stretch to new uncharted areas of your brain. Commit yourself to great achievements, and make this the year to remember!

> "Man alone, of all the creatures of the earth, can change his own pattern. Man alone is the architect of his destiny. The greatest discovery in our generation is that human beings, by changing the inner attitudes of their minds, can change the outer aspects of their lives."
> —**William James**

"Always do right. This will gratify some people and astonish the rest."

—Mark Twain

FRANK M. BASILE
Charisma Publications, Inc.
49 Horseshoe Lane
Carmel, Indiana 46032
(317) 844-0719 ● (317) 844-6067

Frank M. Basile

Frank Basile is Vice-President of the Gene Glick Management Corporation with responsibility for the company's 20,000 apartments and 600 employees in 13 states.

He has conducted over 300 workshops and seminars during the last four years for all types of businesses and organizations from coast to coast, including lectures at several universities, on various subjects—motivation, goal setting, time management, human relations, personal growth, stress, communications, sales, management and real estate management.

He holds the designation of Certified Speaking Professional (CSP), a designation awarded by the National Speakers Association (NSA). He serves as President of the Indiana Chapter of NSA.

He has authored seven books, including Come Fly with Me. He writes a management column for Indianapolis Business Journal and Indiana Business magazine. He has written feature articles and columns for numerous national and regional publications such as Marketing Times, official publication of Sales and Marketing Executives International.

Basile is Chairman of the Board of Indianapolis Sales and Marketing Executives, President of Indianapolis Free University, former President of the Apartment Association of Indiana and former Vice President of the National Apartment Association.

He is a graduate of Tulane University in New Orleans and is listed in Who's Who In the Midwest and Who's Who In Real Estate.

"I'd rather be flying"

BEYOND THE CARROT AND THE WHIP
by Frank M. Basile

"Goal setting is the strongest human force for self motivation."
—Earl Nightingale

What Is Motivation?

I feel very strongly about motivation because it permeates literally everything we do in every area of our lives. And, the extent of our motivation strongly influences how well we do in whatever we do and, in the final analysis, how much happiness we derive from living. It is a very relevant and always timely topic.

I've been concerned with the subject of motivation for about 15 years as a special interest hobby and, in practical application, as an integral part of my business and personal life. My ideas and theories have evolved from my own personal experience, as well as studied observation of other people's experience.

I believe theory should be proven on the crucible of experience. Not philosophical, but practical; not theoretical, but nonetheless, theoretically sound. I want to share with you my personal feelings about motivation. I probably will not say anything new or original; you've heard this before, perhaps said a little differently. Even other chapters of this book will give different insights into the subject of motivation. But, we learn through repetition and perhaps I'll stimulate some additional thoughts, maybe an idea you can use, or encourage you to motivate yourself to some desirable action. That, of course, is where the payoff is.

As Johann Goethe, the German writer and poet said, "The greatet genius will never be worth much if he pretends to draw exclusively from his own resources. What is genius but the faculty of seizing and turning to account everything that strikes us? Every one of my writings has been furnished me by a thousand different persons, a thousand different things."

Therefore, in what I'm about to say, I lay no claim to originality. However, I hope I'm not like the student who made a speech and received the following critique from his speech teacher. "I found your speech to be good and original," she said. "However, the part that was good was not original and the part that was original was not good."

They say when you steal an idea or lift notes from a particular source it's plagiarism, but when you steal from many sources it's known as research. Or, as someone else said, "Originality is the art of concealing your sources." You can be assured that I have stolen from only the best in my research.

What is motivation? Basically, motivation is knowing where you want to go and how you're going to get there. In other words, having a goal and a plan. The derivatives of motivation are motive and action. Goal directed action. They say success is a journey and if you want to go from one place to another you must know where it is you want to go.

After I had been in the motivation field for about ten years, it finally occurred to me to look up the dictionary definition of motivation and see what Webster had to say. I was really quite concerned, because I didn't know what I was going to do if I was wrong after all this time. But, as it turned out, I was quite pleased because Webster agreed with me. And, I'm sure he would have been pleased to know that. Webster's definition is this: Motivation is "that within the individual, rather than without, which incites him to action."

Motivation is not a sales rally—like the sales manager who holds a big sales rally to motivate his salespeople. So what happens? Right after the rally they go to the closest bar or movie to spend the afternoon.

Motivation is not esoteric or mysterious. It's not a big promotion. There's a lot of talk these days about motivation, but not much understanding. It reminds me of a team that won a big game and went to a local bar to celebrate.

The bartender asked one of the players, "What do you attribute the team's success to?" The player replied, without hesitation, "Motivation." The bartender said, "What position does he play?"

Maybe He's A Thoroughbred

From a historical standpoint, the first type of motivation known to man was **FEAR.** The caveman with the biggest club was the motivator. We use that to a great extent today. We threaten to fire somebody if he doesn't perform his job as we want or we threaten to spank our child if he doesn't clean his room.

The classic example is a donkey pulling the cart. We've got a whip, so he's going to pull the cart because of fear of punishment. This type of motivation is only temporary because it is external. It comes from outside of the individual. Soon a person becomes immune to that type of motivation and doesn't react at all.

Later, we got a little more sophisticated with **REWARD MOTIVATION,** which is prevalent in business today. In this case, the donkey is pulling a cart with a carrot dangling from a stick in front of him. He's chasing the carrot and pulling the cart. But, after a while, we have to give him a bite of the carrot or he becomes discouraged. When we give him a bite of the carrot, we destroy the equation and then he's not as hungry anymore. So, we need a bigger carrot, a shorter stick and a lighter load. We're then paying more and more for less and less. Today's fringe benefits are yesterday's incentives. Again, this type of motivation is also temporary, because it comes from outside of the individual.

The only permanent type of motivation is that which

comes from within the individual. It's based on **ATTITUDE**. He's performing because he wants to and not because of the threat of punishment or the promise of reward. When we throw away the whip and get rid of the stick and the carrot, we may find that the donkey is actually a thoroughbred and runs because he wants to.

We are motivated and will do our best *and* have the most fun, when we are doing whatever we are doing because we *want* to do it and not because of fear or reward.

Because we are motivated internally by those things which are important to us, this is permanent motivation. Motivation based upon a reward and/or fear is external and is, therefore, only temporary. The strongest motivation is that which comes from within, which results from setting goals that reflect our basic values.

True motivation goes beyond the carrot and the whip to the goals a person sets for himself. These are what motivate a person to his highest potential and his greatest happiness.

It Is Not Enough to be Busy

Motivation begins with an identification of our values and priorities. Next, we must select specific goals that reflect that value structure. We must then develop a plan of action and a timetable for implementation of each goal. Finally, we must "test" the goal to determine if the benefits of the goal are worth the price we must pay in terms of the plan of action necessary to accomplish the goal. If the answer is "yes," we will automatically generate the necessary desire, self-confidence and determination to carry through with the plan of action.

In addition, when we set goals that reflect our internal value structure, we are doing those things that we most enjoy doing and are most likely to be successful and happy in their pursuit. Will Rogers said, "To be successful in selling or in any other activity in life, you need to know what you are doing, love what you are doing and believe what you are doing." If we are doing that which we enjoy and want to do, we will then take the necessary time and effort to acquire the knowledge and skills for success in that endeavor.

As a byproduct of the identification of our values and goals, we will make the time necessary to accomplish those goals by eliminating activities, people and organizations which do not contribute toward their accomplishment. Henry David Thoreau said, "It is not enough to be busy, the question is what are we busy about." With goals, we know.

Success and Happiness

Success is different things to different people. That is why it is important that the goals we set reflect our own personal value structure. In examining our values, we should consider all areas of our lives, even though not all will be equally important. We will then be in a position to make conscious decisions concerning our personal priorities and what we covet and treasure most—love, friendship, power, fame, fortune, family, pursuit of a hobby, work, career, etc. In other words, we must determine what it is that turns us on. What it is that makes life worth living! What it is that makes us excited about getting up in the morning and looking forward to each new day as a challenge and an opportunity!

Success is the progressive realization of personal goals. Happiness is something to do, somebody to love and something to look forward to—"something to look forward to" are our goals. Goals play a major part in both definitions and are, therefore, essential to success *and* happiness.

The Change Vehicle

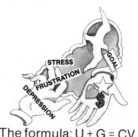

The formula: U + G = CV
(You + Goal = Change Vehicle)

Because of my seminars, workshops and books, I have been called the "Change Vehicle." However, the person himself actually brings about the change in his personality, destiny, actions, habits, thinking, etc. I am only the catalyst who helps a person recognize the need for examining and clarifying his values and then setting specific goals to reflect those values. At that point, the benefits of the goal will motivate him to make the change. The vehicle, therefore, is really the person himself through the goal setting device. I am only the change agent.

People change themselves through goal setting with a little help from an agent who motivates them to recognize their values and set goals. People need guidance to begin this process. If we can somehow motivate a person to analyze his values and set goals, he will do the rest.

This is the reason I conclude each of my programs with a "call to action," requesting that each person set at least one specific goal with a plan of action and timetable. Enthusiasm and excitement can have a lasting carryover effect by translating it into specific goal setting action. Then successes derived through accomplishment of the goals will keep the person enthusiastic on an ongoing basis.

One of the unique features of my seminars is the use of a specially designed 3x5 goal setting card which I distribute at the conclusion. I ask each person to set one goal as a result of the program, write it out in the appropriate blanks on the card and carry it with him or her in pocket or purse as a reminder of the goal until it is accomplished.

When I first began conducting university courses several years ago, I covered primarily the theory and practical application of motivation and why people should set goals. My expectation and request was that each person return home and reflect on his values and set goals. Unfortunately, this latter action, in most cases, never occurred.

I made "survey" phone calls from time to time to research how well the goals were set and the results. I found that hardly anyone had done as they had said. They never set goals. Apparently, when they returned to the "jungle," all of their good intentions faded away with phone calls, drop-in visitors and other routine demands.

I realized that if any change were to take place as a result of this program, action must be taken prior to the conclusion of the program while the excitement and mutual enthusiasm were motivating factors. That's when I began having each person reflect on his values and set some specific goals *during* the class.

We learn through repetition but we learn even faster when we take action. Therefore, if I could get people into motion quickly on the goal setting technique, the chances of their carrying it into their everyday lives were much greater. This reasoning proved correct. The end product of any education must be to stimulate action in the direction of that education. We are much more likely to take action when we take the first step as a part of the program itself.

As a result, my follow-up phone calls during the last several years as well as phone calls and letters from former students, have shown the wisdom of setting goals during the class. In fact, I now have each person set a short-range goal at the conclusion of the first class with volunteer reports at the second class. These initial "successes" with goal setting by class members, most of whom have never set goals before, stimulate the other class members to set goals at the conclusion of that second class. There is nothing like enthusiasm generated through success to encourage not only the successful person, but also those who have heard his "testimony," to get on the goal setting bandwagon. The effects have been phenomenal.

To allow class members to "test the water," we provide a goal setting card and encourage each to set a goal which he can accomplish during the week between classes. As I mentioned, they then report on their experiences at the second class. Whether they report or not, the point is that they will have had a successful, short-term goal setting experience which is likely to motivate them to engage in the full goal setting experience during the second class.

Many positive results come to mind. There was a young lady who confided to the group that she wanted to be a supervisor in her department but had never taken any action. At the conclusion of the first class, she wrote on her goal card that she would take the first step toward becoming a supervisor by discussing her aspirations with her department manager.

At the beginning of the second class, she excitedly reported that her department manager was receptive, encouraged her to proceed with her ambition and provided guidance and support. She received a recommended course of action which included specific courses designed to improve her skills as well as immediate additional responsibility. She was excited because she had taken that all-important first step toward her goal and had gotten direction and encouragement in that endeavor. (P.S. She received that promotion six months later!)

If we get a person, through the vehicle of goal setting, to take that first step and taste the sweet nectar of initial success, it may be all the impetus he needs to continue the process.

I do emphasize to my students, however, that motivation and enthusiasm must be ongoing. It is not sufficient to have a temporary boost even though it has the continuing impetus of goal setting. We must continue to feed our minds with positive input through associating with positive people, reading good books and listening to cassette tapes. I provide information and recommendations of books and tapes.

Goal Cards

The problem with most motivational seminars is that they have a temporary uplifting effect upon the participants with an inevitable letdown as the "high" wears off. There is no carryover, lasting impact unless some action is taken to sustain the enthusiasm. I can achieve this through motivating them to set their goal immediately after the program which will give them the impetus to continue their enthusiasm because of their desire to achieve the goal. Once that goal is achieved, the resulting success feeling, as well as the additional enthusiasm, will hopefully encourage them to continue goal setting.

I believe the real payoff of any educational program comes from doing something a little different than would have been done had it not been for the program. That difference is the goal. Unless we provide the means or device to make it easy for the participants to set goals, the likelihood of their taking any action is practically nil. Psychologists and other analysts tell us that people will forget 95 percent of what was covered in the program unless they take immediate action on the ideas presented or unless they are exposed to repetition.

An additional benefit is the feedback which I get from people who have achieved a goal they would not have achieved had it not been for my program and the goal setting card. Like the person who finally made the decision after many years to go back to school or the person whose sales increased 25 percent.

For me, that kind of feedback is my payoff. It is a "win/win" proposition for all concerned—the members of the audience and me.

Following is a reprint of the goal card which I use to conclude most of my motivational talks:

"GOAL SETTING IS THE STRONGEST
HUMAN FORCE FOR SELF-MOTIVATION"

GOAL
_____

TIMETABLE
_____

PLAN OF ACTION
_____
_____
_____

FRANK BASILE
(317) 844-0719 • P.O. BOX 40321 • INDIANAPOLIS, IN 46240

Direction to Our Dreams

The difference between the disciplined achiever and the average person is not generally superior intellect, ability or skill, but the *use* which each person makes of his talents and abilities. As John Locke once said, "We are born with faculties and powers capable of almost anything, such as at least would carry us further than can be easily imagined; but it is only the *exercise* of those powers which gives us ability and skill in anything and leads us toward perfection."

Goals give direction to our dreams and help channel our energy and resources. We are, therefore, more likely to achieve those things which are important to us and our families and to become the type of person we want. Likewise, in a business enterprise, we are more likely to effectively utilize our limited resources (time, capital, manpower, equipment) when we have specific goals which then allow us to channel those resources directly to the goal.

Imagine a series of arrows, which represent our energy, experience, creativity, know-how and time we have available. Without goals, our talents and energy are disbursed. We're like a wandering generality. Our arrows are going in every direction and lose effectiveness. If we accomplish anything at all, it is by accident and probably not what we would have chosen had we consciously thought about it. However, when we have clearly defined goals, our resources are in perfect alignment. There is a clean thrust. It is like using a giant magnifying glass to focus the sun's rays on a single spot. The result is an intensity which can remove obstacles to accomplishing any goal we choose.

But, we spend more time planning our vacations than our lives. A business owner wouldn't think of operating without a profit objective and an operating plan, which is called the budget.

It is a generally accepted fact that the average

person uses only about 20 percent of his potential. Einstein said he used only 15 percent of his. Consider what you would do with a clock that operated at only 20 percent efficiency. You would probably throw it away. Goals don't increase a person's potential but, just as importantly, they increase the percentage utilization. We don't want to be like the old farmer who was invited to attend a community meeting on new farming techniques. He declined, saying, "I don't farm half as good as I know how now."

99 Percent Increase

In 1980, I reluctantly accepted the position of chairman of my company's United Way campaign. After accepting this responsibility, I decided to put myself completely into it on my personal belief that if a job is worth doing, it is worth doing well. As you would expect, I applied goal setting to the task.

With the assistance of the personnel department, I recapped the past year's activity by department—including number of persons within each department, number who contributed, percentage participation, amount contributed, amount contributed per capita, etc. I then developed departmental objectives by considering last year's performance by department and the overall desired company goal for this year.

I asked each department manager to accept responsibility for his department's share of the overall company goal and provided each with a recap of last year's performance and this year's objectives.

I also provided each department manager with a

suggested plan of action but allowed him to modify it to his personality and department since the results were his responsibility.

Our company achieved a 99 percent increase over the prior year, which performance had been satisfactory. As a result, we were among the few in the city who received United Way's highest award—the Gold Award of Excellence. This award requires a minimum level of 80 percent of full giving potential.

This demonstrates the power of goal setting to change a satisfactory performance to an outstanding one! The cast of players was the same but goal setting made all the difference.

United Way solicitation has continued with the same procedure of setting goals and developing an individual departmental plan of action. Only the amount of the goal has changed to keep pace with the overall needs of the United Way agencies. We accomplished our share of that goal again in 1981 and 1982.

Weight Loss

During my annual physical examination, my physician recommended that I lose 20 pounds. About four months later, I visited the office because of a sprained wrist. His nurse weighed me, as is their procedure. She asked, "Are you sick?" I replied, "No, except for the wrist which is the reason I am here." She said, "You've had a big weight loss in the last few months." I said, "That's right." I reminded her that the doctor had recommended that I lose 20 pounds.

At that point, she was re-reading my file which included the physical examination report and looked rather quizzical. I asked if there was anything wrong. She said, "No, only that the doctor makes this recommendation quite frequently but hardly anybody actually loses the weight!"

As a postscript to that little story, I have kept the weight off by using a goal-directed plan of action. In this case, the plan did not include one of the fad diets. I started to eat sensible, balanced meals, cutting down on foods that I like but I know are fattening, such as bread and dessert. I have now returned to eating those types of food but in moderation.

The primary thrust was to reduce the intake by "dieting." The second half of the action plan to lose weight was to begin an exercise program to burn calories and tone-up my body.

I started the Royal Canadian Air Force exercise program. I had to talk myself into doing it because I do not enjoy exercising. However, I kept reminding myself of the benefits and the results of the exercising to date: feeling good, being in shape, maintaining my weight and being healthier.

As with any goal, we should reduce it to short-term goals and maintain the discipline of daily action. This is exemplified in an exercise program where daily action is the cornerstone of the entire program.

One of the little "tricks" that I use to keep me on a daily routine is short-term interim rewards. For example, I might put the coffee on when I wake up at 6:00 a.m. After I have completed one-third of the exercises, I treat myself to a cup (while continuing to exercise). I then turn on the television as a distraction from the relatively boring exercise routine which makes it easier to accomplish the goal. Or, I listen to a cassette tape of information or motivational material.

I needed greater discipline at the beginning to get into the exercise habit but, as I mentioned, it still takes constant reminding of the benefits to be gained by that sacrifice or "price" (which is the plan of action). However, once the routine became habit, it required fewer short-term rewards and daily pep talks. It takes discipline to acquire a new good habit, such as an exercise routine, but, once acquired, it begins operating out of the subconscious more or less automatically. It becomes internalized and requires less conscious discipline and thought as time goes on.

We should make a decision up front as to whether we truly want to lose weight. We should analyze the benefits of weight loss such as looking more attractive, perhaps living longer, getting compliments from our friends, having clothes fit better, feeling better, etc.

We should then analyze the price we must pay which is the plan of action necessary to accomplish the weight loss goal. This would include: no late evening meals, an exercise program, improved eating habits, etc.

If we decide that the benefits of losing weight are worth the price, then we will be motivated to take action. Otherwise, if we decide that a loss in weight is not worth the price, we can forget about the goal and not feel guilty about being overweight.

In programming a weight loss, we should set interim short-term goals to support the long-term objective of the overall desired weight loss. For example, if we merely said we wanted to lose 15 pounds in three months, and only lost one or two pounds the first week or perhaps five pounds during the first two weeks, we might become discouraged. The long term goal is not sufficient to maintain our overall enthusiasm.

However, if we said we would lose two pounds the first week, three pounds the second week, one pound the third week and so on, each time we accomplished our short-term goal, we would have positive "success" feedback which would continue our enthusiasm.

These short-term goals, which provide interim positive feedback, are necessary to keep us excited and enthusiastic about the long-term goal and making all of the interim sacrifices.

Dealer Partners

When I was with a large automobile manufacturer many years ago, there was a dealership in the largest town in my zone which had historically been one of the poorest sales performers in the company. However, I knew this dealership had a great potential for improvement, partially because they were getting such a relatively small share of the market.

After I was assigned to that zone for a couple of months, there was still no improvement. It performed as it always had—very poorly. From time to time, I made recommendations to one or the other of the two dealer partners to take some action such as changing advertising, revising the salesmen compensation program, ordering a different assortment of cars, changing sales managers, etc. I would leave the dealership, never knowing if the agreed upon action would be taken. The partner I had spoken with would talk with the other and perhaps change what we had decided in our earlier meeting. As a result, there was no progress and I became quite frustrated.

Finally, one day I checked into the hotel where I stayed when I was in that town and phoned one of the partners. I asked that he meet me at the hotel. He said that he conducts his business at the dealership and wanted to meet me there. I asked that he come to the hotel for a brief meeting just this one time.

I asked that he bring his partner with him. He said that he could come but his partner was tied up in the service department that afternoon. I said I would prefer to wait until that evening when both were available so I could talk with them at the same time. They reluctantly agreed and came to my room that evening.

I asked each to write on a blank sheet of paper what he expected out of the dealership or, more specifically, his goals for the dealership. They said they knew why they were in the dealership and didn't see why this exercise was necessary. I asked them to do this one thing.

For two people who supposedly knew why they each had $100,000 invested in the business, it took them several minutes before they began writing. After they finally finished, I put the two pages side by side to compare them. They had nothing in common. None of the goals were the same!

One wanted cash flow on a regular basis and other so-called objectives. The other, being wealthy, wanted tax shelter and an opportunity to offset his substantial income from other enterprises such as banking and cattle. He was interested in capital appreciation over the long run with minimum interim income.

I then advised them that I was going to return to the District Office and immediately recommend that their franchise be cancelled unless one bought out the other. They became quite upset and I left almost immediately before violence ensued. After they determined that I was serious in what I was going to do, one did buy out the other.

Now, I was dealing with one person with one goal and one plan of action. As I had anticipated, sales increased substantially almost immediately.

As a result, that dealership, which had never been higher than #150 out of 175 dealers in the district, became #1 in the district, sales as a percent of objective, within 45 days! In ten of the next twelve months, they were #1. As a result, I won trips to Las Vegas, London and Hawaii in sales contests.

I use this illustration to point out what can happen when we have a single goal, as compared to hazy, undefined and conflicting goals. Not only did the partners not have compatible goals but they didn't have goals at all. Therefore, with such tremendous untapped potential, when a single goal was established along with a plan of action and timetable, they took off like a rocket.

This again demonstrates the change potential of goal setting.

Winning Contests

During my 12 years with a large automobile manufacturer, I won more than my share of contests. My basic formula was to set goals, develop a plan of action and establish timetables for each contest immediately after it was announced. The goals were designed to ensure victory. I calculated what I thought was needed to win, i.e., unit sales, dollar volume, etc. I then wrote out the plan of action along with the timetable.

I also wrote down the contest award which was cash, merchandise and/or a trip. The benefits of winning the contest became a constant motivator. The benefits revolved around whatever the contest award was. Incidentally, I found I could motivate myself better when the award was a trip. I would put exotic pictures of the trip award destination on my refrigerator at home, on the bulletin board over my desk, and on the dashboard of my car. When the going got rough and I was tempted to question whether I should push and make still another dealer call that evening or work until 8:00 p.m. each night, the picture reminded me of the reward I was seeking. This was the motivator!

The point is that it should be something specific that you can visualize and, therefore, fix in your subconscious mind. If the award were cash, I would think of what I could buy and that would become the motivating factor. If the award were merchandise, I would visualize using it. I tried to focus on the benefits for obtaining the objective which, in this case, was winning the contest. I then developed a detailed plan of action designed to win.

As an example of the action plan, I would "break down" my overall zone sales objective to my 12 to 15 dealers comprising the zone. This would establish their individual goals for me to reach the overall goal. I then visited each dealer and asked him to accept the objective or perhaps set his own objective, which would hopefully be higher than what I needed from him to win the contest.

He and I would then develop a plan of action designed to accomplish his individual objective. In this way, we had a series of objectives whereby each dealer, instrumental in the overall objective, would agree upon the objective and plan of action designed to ensure the overall victory of the zone.

Therefore, I had an agreement with each dealer on his goal and plan of action. Everyone on my team not only knew what his share of the job was but exactly how he could accomplish it. And, he was committed because it was his goal and his plan.

This is another illustration of the power of goal setting in achieving whatever it is that success means to us. In those days, success for me included winning those contests.

Punchline

I am going to ask you to set one goal before you go to sleep tonight. This is the "punch line" of all my motivational talks. Commit to yourself that you will do this and write it down on a 3x5 card. It doesn't have to be some far-reaching goal. Maybe something you have been thinking about for a while and never got around to. But, just one. Not a bunch of New Year's resolutions.

But don't do like the fellow who attended one of my programs a couple of years ago. He did as I requested and wrote his goal on a card. However, instead of taking it with him, he left it in the meeting room. It would not have done him any good anyway because on his card he had written, "My goal: I want to be happy by Tuesday afternoon."

I don't believe I need to tell you that is not goal setting. That is wishful thinking. The question is, "What is it specifically that will make us happier, more successful, more fulfilled?" The more specific, the better. When we are specific, we are able to visualize the goal and be more specific in the plan of action.

Keep the card in your pocket or purse as a reminder of your goal until it is accomplished. Then set another goal until goal setting becomes a habit. Emerson said, "We form habits, then our habits form us."

This can be the "first day of the rest of your life." The journey of a thousand miles begins with a single step. We can take that step today, so we don't end up like the guy whose epitaph read, "He asked little of life and life paid his price."

My wish for you is not that you work longer or harder, but rather shorter, more productive hours toward the attainment of your personal and professional goals.

Putting it all together

SUSAN HAMILTON JOHNSON
Susan Hamilton Associates
8 Powderhorn
Little Rock, AR 72205
(501) 227-8880

Susan Hamilton Johnson

Susan Johnson is a motivator of people and an inspiration to those who meet her. Susan definitely possesses the "magic." Her success lies in her belief in herself, her direction and her contribution to life—to help others realize their dreams. When others ask why, Susan asks why not?

Through determination and drive Susan proved herself early as the youngest retail buyer in the country. At age 22 she was an executive of a national multimillion dollar department store with a purchasing responsibility of $1.5 million. Her aggressive business sense moved her rapidly through several major chain stores, as well as domestic and international markets.

Susan retired from the retail business in 1977 but not from the industry. She moved permanently to New York, attended the New York School of Interior Design and opened Hamilton Interiors where she converted unappealing showroom interiors to dazzling showplaces for fashion merchandise.

Susan married and moved to Little Rock where she pursued her dream—to share with others the success formula which had worked for her. Susan's successful speaking career has brought her in front of thousands to share her success secrets. She is a platform speaker, trainer, author, college faculty member and columnist.

Susan believes the ability to achieve success and realize our dreams lies in each of us, but as Peter Pan said, "As people grow old, they lose the magic." Susan helps remember the magic and unlock the talent hidden inside each of us.

BATTER UP!
by Susan Hamilton Johnson

"I want to help you to grow as beautiful as God meant you to be when he thought of you first."

—George MacDonald

Each morning the umpire cries, "Batter up!" I look around and I'm always next—wow—another chance to hit a homer. I'm wearing my new starched uniform, the crowd roars and I step into the batter's box. Today's the day. I can feel it. I know it's gonna be a winner! Each day is a step towards realizing goals and fulfilling potential. What a magnificent challenge lies ahead. I'm lucky, I learned the success principles early. I know that to be successful at anything I do I must step up to the bat continually—ready to give it my best shot. I've grounded out, struck out, then hit a homer, the reward for being willing to take a chance.

Many people say luck doesn't enter into success, maybe I'm the exception. I'm lucky, I learned my lessons early and was taught by the best. I have usually been in the right place at the right time. I have paid the dues, learned the game plan, put it all together and made it happen. That's the thrilling part of the challenge. I can make it happen every hour, every day, every month, every year. I know where I want to go, what I will accomplish and the price I must pay. Realistic goal setting? You bet your boots, without it I would be lost. Every time I come to bat prepared, armed with the facts, great self-assurance and looking good—guess what, I hit the homer. Not surprising—I knew I would. Not luck but practice. I knew what had to be done to hit a winner, what price had to be paid.

Step Up and Take A Chance!

Yes, I have been successful, am sucessful today and will be successful tomorrow. I know who I am, what my strengths are, where I am going and how long it will take —realistically. Realistic goal setting is the only way I can measure my progress. I must be able to reflect on a day, a week or a month and see the progress.

So many people give up just before they reach the top; many give up before they ever get going. Why? Because so many try to do it all this week, they take on too much and fail to set realistic goals that will lead them to success. I know I will be successful because I am willing to learn new skills, develop my talent and pay the price. I know what I will do once I cross home plate.

What is that one unique factor that makes me different from all the rest? What do I do better than anyone else, what makes me special—what will be my contribution? I am willing to *take the chance,* a chance at success. The gamble has paid off. I have developed not one but three successful careers. As a buyer and executive for major department stores, my responsibilities included purchases worth several millions of dollars, advertising schedules, budget planning, international purchasing and buying responsibilities for as many as twelve branch stores. As an interior designer in New York, my clients were leading manufacturers in the garment center and Park Avenue residents. I was invited to participate in several prestigious designer showhouses. Now as a platform speaker, business consultant, author and college teacher, I research and write my own material, and handle the marketing and public relations for both Susan Johnson Associates and Johnson/Wimberley.

Behind every success story there are reasons why. Like a winning team no one player is the only star. Success has coaches, equipment, practice, players and fans. Remember with every success, every winning team, there are 10, 100 or 1,000 attempts and failures; nothing comes overnight. It comes through diligence and hardwork. When we meet successful people we want to know how they did it; what worked for them? How can it work for us? I would like to share with you a few of my success secrets, what keeps me motivated and how I have seen it work for others. I hope just one idea can help you advance and enrich your life.

First Base!

At college graduation my father shook my hand, gave

me a gold watch as his father had given him. That was the unspoken challenge; time for me to take hold of my life. The training period was over, this was the real game. At last, it was my time to make a contribution. I graduated from the University of Arkansas with a degree in History. Wow! What now? The only jobs I seemed qualified for were receptionist positions, and even that was questionable. A friend suggested I interview with a major department store chain, Dillard's. The store was expanding and interviewing for buyer trainee positions. I certainly had nothing to lose. The fashion industry was fascinating. Little did I know such a fantastic career awaited. The day of the interview I knew the feeling a rookie batter has as he steps up to the plate for the first inning of a series game. The butterflies were everywhere but, I felt great, I looked great and I was exhilarated at the thought of selling me! No one could sell me better than I could. I knew I would convince him I could do the job. I was selling myself and loving it! I walked in, filled with ambition, positive self-esteem and a willingness to work. I sold myself—the position was mine! I was thrilled at the prospect of working 48 hours a week in return for $400 per month!

I immediately found the challenges exciting. For the first time I was given responsibility, decision making tasks, and management of others. My goals were measured daily by sales figures. I worked far more than forty-eight hours a week, eager to learn every facet of the business. I was lucky; of all the coaches, the first was to be Ernie Long, a gentleman who carried dignity and respect throughout the industry. In my seven years in the business, no one ever measured his professionalism. His true love for the business, professional attitude and gift of teaching helped lay a strong foundation for my promising career. I realized quickly the interdependence and respect we had for one another. A successful business, like a winning team, operates not just on the talents of one but of many. The team worked well and within 15 months I was promoted to the buying position for Sleepwear and Robes, a sizeable area with a sales volume of well over one million dollars. More challenges, more goals, more successes. I had learned much from Ernie; organization, honesty, the facts and how to's of buying—I entered the New York market for the first time in August, 1972 with something special. Ernie had taught me above all— be a lady and be a professional.

Looking Like A Winner!

I was young, 23 years old and representing a major department store doing business in five states. The "buying pencil," well over a million dollars, was definitely not the minor leagues. I realized quickly my youth was a drawback. I also knew that as I had done in the job interview, my ability to sell myself was now my strength. Long before John Malloy's book *Dress for Success* was published, I was applying those principles to marketing my exterior. To be regarded as a professional, I knew I had to look like a professional. I purchased two suits, the best I could afford and began to adopt a professional look and attitude. It worked! I had followed in Ernie's path. He was proud of me and I was proud of myself. Looking like a professional may have helped get an appointment with the right manu-facturer; however, it did not make the daily sales figures. Those figures are the barometer of success or failure for every buyer. Looking the part or not, the buying decisions had to be professional.

On Base With A Single!

The industry took note of this rookie buyer and soon there were offers from other stores. After all, the figures didn't lie.   A 23-year-old was doubling sales figures, lowering costs and increasing profits. That gets attention! After a short 15-month buying period with Dillard's, the offer came I could not refuse. Rich's, Atlanta, one of the country's leading ten retailers, wanted to interview me for the position of Sleepwear Buyer. I met with everyone from the President to the Merchandise Manager.I was back in the position of selling myself. I loved it! The figures backed my success, now came the fun of selling me. I knew I would be successful, I had already envisioned myself as the youngest buyer for a major store in the country. There would surely be magazine articles, interviews, talk shows, WOW! Whatever their needs, this whiz kid could double figures, set it straight and be a star. With the new territory came frequent trips to New York, catalogue selection and purchases, plus an introduction to the complex world of importing. I have always learned from those who teach, and here I learned survival! After two days into the job, I realized I was too green for the amount of responsibility. Could I make the team—or get cut midseason? My choice. I had the "stuff," now could I prove it? This "hotshot young super buyer" had oversold herself and the future of a career lay in the outcome.

The market place had raved, "Susan crackles! A live wire with enthusiasm and direction! Susan makes it happen!!" I had sold myself despite the tremendous lack of experience—I had won the inning but could lose the game. Now was the time to deliver! This was the major leagues. They would not tolerate a rookie. Sales figures were dropping, the market place became unsure of my ability. Like a shark they sensed someone wounded and moved in for the kill. Their business was also at stake. They would do what was necessary to protect it. The inevitable came two short weeks from my first day at the store. I was called into *the* office and placed on a 30-day probation. A simple mandate. Deliver increased sales or resign. With a million dollar volume at stake there is no mincing of words. The message was direct. A strike out and the game would be over.

Return To The Basics: Analyze Your Strengths!

I took a long, hard look and knew I had to evaluate my strengths. When all else fails and self-doubt sets in, I return to the drawing board. It seems that whenever I have faltered or lost self-confidence it was because I was operating away from my power base, away from what I do best, out of my comfort zone. As long as I am doing what I know I do best, then I perform at my peak level. Recently when addressing the sales force for I.B.M., I challenged each individual to analyze his or her own strengths. Ask others for their opinion. Sometimes we confuse what we would like to believe are our strengths with what they truly are.

Others recognize qualities we didn't know we had. I believe we cannot possibly decide where we are going until we first know not only who we are but what is our unique contribution. Ask yourself, what do I do better than anyone else? What would I like to be doing? What am I willing to do to get there? Successful people know what their strengths are, what they do better than anyone else. Do you remember Mickey Mantel for his hitting or fielding abiltiy? How about Yogi Berra—catching or base running? We remember each one for his strength. Yes, they were all-around good athletes—but there was that one very special talent. So on a piece of paper I suggest the following:

1) List your strengths.

2) List your goals: long and short term.

3) What is your contribution?

We are each individuals with many talents, some more developed than others. It takes time to honestly evaluate and decide who you are, where you are going and what you plan to do once you get there. By writing it, the plan is reinforced. Those thoughts and dreams become more real when you can look at them. It takes time. It isn't easy. Some never have the answers, but those are the ones who never try. Believe me, NO successful person has achieved fame without answering all three questions. Who am I? Where am I going? and

WHY?

At the State Convention for Hospital Administrative Secretaries, a woman patiently waited while I shook hands with many at the conclusion of the program. She said, "Susan, I just don't have any special talent or contribution, I'm just a housewife and a secretary." My heart cried for her analysis of herself. I told her that she had not dug deep enough and that I bet she had never given herself the time or the *right* to find herself. Talent must be unearthed, cultivated and nourished—nothing in this world comes easily. Would we want it if it did? All that is worth having is certainly worth working for, otherwise it is meaningless.

I challenged her to read two books, *Release Your Brakes* by Jim Newman and *As A Man Thinketh* by James Allen. I gave her a list of five questions that required much thought and made her promise to call me in a week. We have spoken almost every week since then. It is exciting to see her life change and a dream become a reality. She had always wanted to be involved with care for the elderly. Recently she finished night school courses for certification and is beginning a new career in geriatric Health Care with many fresh creative ideas. What a talent that could have been lost! She acknowledged her desire, developed her talent, acquired the skill and now her dream is real! That's success!!

The Time To Deliver!

With my buying position at Rich's in jeopardy, not to mention my career, I returned to the drawing board to analyze my strengths. I realized that for the first two weeks I had worked from my weaknesses—focusing on the overwhelming task ahead and all that I did not know instead of all that I did know. Once I realized that I was not operating from my power base I was able to get back on track. What I had sold the company, ME—I was simply not delivering. The problem didn't lie within the complexity of the job—it lay within myself! I was working with my brakes on! By no means was I living up to my potential. I would change my attitude, I would be back on top, I would come to bat and hit that home run. I would not be denied!

I dug deeper, stayed later, came in earlier, worked weekends, learned and relearned every procedure. I was in the fight of my life. I suffered from fatigue and nervous exhaustion but I would not give up. The 30 days were up. The month-end figures printed. As I quickly scanned the computer printout to the bottom figure, the excitement mounted—the sound of the crack of the bat as the ball sailed out of the park—the pounding of my heart as I rounded the bases. Wow, I could feel it all! The sales figures had responded. The decisions made were right. I had met the challenge and WON!

Inning Change!

I worked for other major stores, Joske's, San Antonio, and Stix, Baer & Fuller, St. Louis. The responsibilities, travel, income and industry respect grew. Each day meant new sales figures, new goals. I continued to move from one failing department to another, being able to enjoy immediate success within 90 days. The sales and profits increased quickly. In 1977, I suffered what I know today to be "career burnout." Something was missing. I had no real interaction with others—everything was reduced to the bottom line, no artistic creativity. As one of the industry's leading and influential women, I left the position, power and prestige to move to New York.

The day I realized I didn't want to get to the office at 7:30 and put in a full twelve-hour day was when I knew it was time to get out. There really was no soul searching decision. The challenge simply was no longer there. At the Independent Insurance Agents Convention, I stressed the need to evaluate our situations regularly. Ask yourself, "Does this challenge me? Do I enjoy it? Do I contribute something? Do I want to do it tomorrow?" If you answer "no" as I did, it's time to move on. I am still made of that winning "stuff" regardless of what career I pursue. No one and no job will ever rob me of my talent.

So again, I analyzed my strengths and what I knew made me successful. I listed only four so I could concentrate my effort. If I spend precious time making weaknesses strong, they run the risk of cracking under pressure; however, if I build my strengths into iron blocks—earthquakes cannot rock that foundation! The following are strengths that have contributed to my success. Perhaps they will help you.

1) *Always* be a professional!

2) *Learn* from the BEST and *teach* what you learn.

3) *Creativity*—find a need and fill it!

4) *Belief*—above all else keep the belief in yourself.

1) Always be a professional. That carries a great deal of responsibility. I consider myself a professional, carry myself as a professional and because of that, I am treated like a professional. I learned early, as the other buyers wore jeans and leisure clothes while travelling, that if I was dressed as a professional, I always received preferred treatment. Cabs were available, porters, bell captains, waiters and others. I have always been very conscious of my appearance and the statement it makes. I was very flattered when, at a recent National Speakers Association Convention, a fellow noted speaker, Patricia Fripp, remarked about my appearance, "Regardless of her current fee structure, Susan 'looks' like a two thousand dollar speaker!" That is proof enough for me. Your image is your calling card. What does it say about you? Being a professional means regarding others with respect. I respect their time and opinion whether they are the boss, an assistant or a client. We are all individuals making our way in this world. The least we deserve is the respect of one another.

2) Learn from the best. At the Arkansas Automobile Dealers Association Convention, I was asked what the main factor was that contributed to my success at such an early age. Simple. I surrounded myself with the best supervisors and assistants. I always had the very best team. When I interviewed for a new position, I didn't just look at the personal challenge, the location and the monetary increase. My number one critique factor was the people. Did I respect their ability, could I learn from them, how strong was the team spirit? I am the product of hundreds of years of trial and error by others. Philosophers, teachers, professionals, role models and friends. I had many who gave me their very best. In turn I passed on my teachings to others. It was my responsibility to help them grow. One of the most rewarding parts of life is to be able to give what you have learned to others. If the circle is complete, then I feel I have the right to return to my mentors in search of more.

3) Creativity. My interpretation is to be flexible in satisfying the needs of others. Remember—you can determine who you are and where you are going, but when you decide what your unique contribution is to be—that's creativity! Creativity is rubber, it moves constantly. When I envision creativity I think of a pinball machine and how the silver ball bounces from side to side almost slipping through, only to be propelled by the flippers for one more opportunity to ring the bell and light the lights. Creativity is the spark that ignites the gas and runs the engine. Creativity is the key to every success. To fill a need, turn a dream into reality or try something new never attempted before—now, that's creativity.

The first public seminar I ever conducted was solely the product of a dream. In the fall of 1980, I realized a need to provide current information to professional women in the areas of developing professional attitudes, time management and effective communications. I knew I could fill the void. I spoke to as many clubs in the metro area as possible. I announced the March date and program agenda while at the same time exposing myself to this new audience and gathering information for future seminars. Like spring training and the hours of practice, the price paid to insure success was time. Countless stuffed tomatoes and club meetings later, the time invested paid off. The seminar was a complete sellout, a capacity crowd of 350!

To be creative is to be innovative. The most original idea is worthless if it is not implemented. You must be willing to make the idea happen—put it into reality. Find others to help me make the dream real. Many times I feel like the whole team: pitcher, batter, shortstop, coach and water boy. For my creativity, my dreams to become reality, I am willing to pay the price. Creativity gives us the *right to try* and maybe even fail, but that's all right because when you possess creativity there is always another chance.

4) Belief—The unquestioning faith of a winner! If I don't believe in myself, no one else will either. Regardless of all else—my belief in me and my contribution must at all times remain strong. Belief is being able to take a chance at success knowing that the odds are in *your* favor because you stacked the deck. The more practice sessions, the more winning is guaranteed. Simple as that. When I truly, deeply believe—when it is imbedded deep in my subconscious—when I can FEEL the victory— THEN it happens! I can fool a lot of people but not my subconscious. I know there's a price to pay—saying it doesn't get the job done. I can confidently walk into the game knowing I will win only when I have followed the winning rules: 1) I must know my strength, 2) I must know my goal, 3) I must know my purpose, and 4) I must know I can do it! Winning is the constant fight to stay on top, never at the expense of others but always pushing the inner boundaries of myself; pushing to learn more, grow more, feel more. Belief, the personal contest that says, "I CAN." That is what challenges us to move forward, experience life and live!

Game Two!

I sold my condominium, sold my car, put my furniture in storage and sent the plants home to Mother. Off I went to New York. In a few days I had disposed of all that took years to acquire. With the excess baggage gone, I arrived in New York with two suitcases that surely weighed 100 pounds each and made my way to the Barbizon Hotel for Women (quite a change from the expense account suite at the Regency Hotel on Park Avenue). I took the subway to the New York School of Interior Design for morning classes and in the afternoon was in the garment center selling myself and my ideas on redesigning showrooms. I was playing on a strength—seven years in the garment center gave me more friends and contacts than most people have in a lifetime. It was my turn to sell them! I knew their business and their needs sometimes better than they did. I found a need and filled it! I had spent countless hours in uncomfortable chairs with carpet colors screaming of 60's Mod Rock and poor lighting. I knew properly designed showrooms would better enhance their merchandise and increase sales. Remember, I listed my #1 strength as being a pro-fessional. I was respected, and although I was entering a new field, my friends were willing to take a chance. They knew I would not come to them until I was ready—ready to do the job, do it right and deliver satisfaction.

I worked hard at the New York School. After all, I had an entire garment center patiently waiting for my talent! School provided facts but I needed more. Back to my strengths, I knew I could not learn the business alone. I needed a teacher, the *best*. I inquired at the school counselor's office and luck of lucks, a top designer, Sandra Merriman, had just called asking for an assistant. The counselor thought we would make a great team. Off I went to meet one of the most beautiful, fascinating and naturally talented women I have ever known. Sandra was a mentor, employer and friend. I grew quickly with her not only in Interior Design but more so emotionally and within myself. We always learn something from some-one, it may not be what we had intended—but each new person holds one new thought or idea for us. Do you share ideas with others so you both will grow? Each of us has gifts to give and receive, yet we never exchange nearly enough.

As planned, business was good, I was an associate of Sandra Merriman, Inc. and opened Hamilton Interiors. My clients were the garment industry and investment renovations. I lived in a luxury brownstone I helped restore on Park Avenue and 79th. I had several close friends, interesting men, limousines, the theater, Europe and the Carribean. Wow, life was grand! The scoreboard was all lit up and I was way ahead. I had New York by the tail and I wouldn't let go. As did all New Yorkers, I left the city early in July to visit friends across the country and return Labor Day. On my return trip I stopped in Little Rock to visit family and, of course, dear, dear Dad. He wanted me to meet someone. He had never asked before and was very persistent. So to appease my dear, dear Dad I met this young attorney, romantically I might add in my father's xerox room. It was not love at first sight but more like two nervous teenagers, with an eventual invitation to dinner. Whatever that young man said it must have been right—we were engaged in seven days and married six weeks later! Needless to say, he was not in favor of moving to New York, so back to the drawing board—time to analyze those strengths again. I moved Hamilton Interiors to Little Rock, shipped a few things home, sold the rest and said goodbye.

Hamilton Interiors opened as a success from the beginning. However, was it really what I wanted to contribute? Was this my unique gift, could I do this better than anyone else? An old friend, Barbara Day, had heard I returned to Little Rock and asked if I would be interested in conducting fashion seminars in the department store. The creative juices began to flow. I realized I had so much information that other working women needed; information I had learned from others, that I took for granted now had new importance. I had been asked to speak to clubs on the topic of success, but this was different, this was *me!* We worked closely and together built a strong seminar following. It was simple and fun, we offered the right information at the right time at the right price. I was soon speaking to audiences in the hundreds and loving every moment.

A member of the National Speakers Association heard

me address the University of Arkansas Business School on the subject of "Professional Awareness." She encouraged me to join and attend the convention. I had never heard of being a professional speaker, much less N.S.A. I attended my first convention three months later and have been involved and loving it ever since. No doubt my success as a speaker will be attributed to two things—the professionalism and teachings of the great speakers at N.S.A., and my personal style and my contribution to the profession.

My business now includes platform speaking, consulting, writing, teaching and direct sales marketing. In my leisure time I am a Bulldogger. (You guessed it—I raise and show English Bulldogs.) The satisfaction I receive from watching a pup grow into a champion contender is tremendous. Life continues to surprise me with many rewards. Despite achievement and success, the greatest challenge is just beginning—that of raising a family and helping a child realize the beauty of this life. I made the choice long ago to love life and live it—WOW—am I glad I did!

GURMIT SINGH
Dynamic Communications International
P.O. Box 1174
Jalan Pantai Baru
Kuala Lumpur, Malaysia
03-566-742

Gurmit Singh

Gurmit Singh was born in 1951 in a small village called Taran Tarn in Punjab, India. He was educated in the largest University in the world called . . . LIFE.

Mr Gurmit's career began in the Transport industry where work was tough and demanding. After two years, he switched over to the Hotel and Catering industry and later went into business for himself in the Import and Export and Mail Order fields. In the process, he also picked up useful and beneficial sales, management and marketing expertise.

Although he has had a strong belief in himself and a very positive outlook all along, it wasn't until he was exposed to the Personal Development Industry in 1975 that he realized his true desire in life was working with and developing people's potential. Today, he is the Founder and President of his own training organization.

He is an associate member of the Malaysian Institute of Personnel Managers, a Rotarian and a member of the prestigious National Speakers Association, U.S.A. His expertise has literally helped thousands of people from all walks of life achieve success in their lives and work. As a businessman, he maintains his interest in World Trade and Real Estate.

His soon to be released book is entitled That Little Extra Effort. *The ideas and thoughts it presents will open up a new world of possibilities to you. Gurmit is a man you just cannot afford to ignore!*

DON'T JUST EXIST— LIVE . . . MAGNIFICENTLY!

by Gurmit Singh

"They can because they think they can."
Vergil-Aeneid

"Be Daring, Be Different, Be First!"

Destination Earth, Mission . . . ?

Millions have come and millions have gone through this lovely world of ours. Many millions more will be taking the next flight into the unknown. When is your flight? Do you know? I don't, but I do happen to know that I came with a nontransferable return ticket and I have to make that return trip someday . . . ANYDAY!

A little frightening, isn't it? I'm sorry, I didn't mean to

worry you, I just wanted to remind you that you did not come here by chance. There is a reason for your being here. When we make a trip or take a flight to any destination, we always do so for a reason, don't we? We either go for a holiday, on business, to visit someone or for a combination of reasons. There is always a purpose. Well, what is your purpose here on earth, my friend?

Let's you and I do one of the most "dangerous" things in the world. Let's think. Let's think about our mission here on earth. Most of us don't know what we want to do here, or worse still, why we were even born in the first place. The trouble is most people don't take the time and effort to consider their objective in life. They just keep existing while complaining and grumbling that life is not giving them their fair share, and then without warning their time is up! With so much potential achievement within man, he often still goes to the grave with his best music still unsung. WHY? WHY? WHY?

Could you sit alone for the next one hour and ask yourself, "What am I doing here and what shall I do with this life of mine?"

Take a note pad and pen and write down all the things that you feel or think you want to do, have or become. As each year passes while you pursue those objectives, new thoughts will come and new plans will have to be made. Go ahead and work towards them, they are *your* plans, remember? Not those of your friends, your parents, or relatives but your very own dreams! You make the choice of keeping them or throwing them away.

From research, study and keen observations of human beings of both sexes, young and old, I have noticed that when their dreams are limited, human beings begin to stagnate. Astonishingly, many people actually give up living because they have nothing left to look forward to anymore. This is common among the older working people who retire after working for 35 years or so. When they have no purpose or goal to work for, they become ill and die within a few years. Those who have a purpose, a dream, a goal towards which they are directing their energies regularly, seem to go on living forever. Nourishing a big dream in our hearts will keep us alive by our very determination to make it come true. Don't ever forget this idea that I am going to share with you.

Don't Let Your Dreams Die; If They Do, So Will You

When one dream is reached, quickly build another. In fact, build several big ones that would require more effort and time on your part to make them come true. Doing so will not make you invincible but it will certainly put you on the right track and in control of yourself at all times. You will be able to pilot your life in any direction that you choose.

There is a purpose in everyone's life. Let's search for it and make the best of whatever it is. If you happen to be a farmer growing crops for humanity, be the very best farmer you can. It's not important for the public to know what you are achieving. The most important fact is that you know you are doing your best. That knowledge will give you a sense of accomplishment, happiness and peace of mind. Isn't that what we all are looking for?

If farming is not making you happy, then reach out for

something more to your liking. It may be a lower paid job or a glamorous one; whatever it may be, *go for it!* It's your life to live and it's your decision to make. The big question at this stage that frightens many people and stops them from taking action is usually "HOW? How can I do it? I don't have enough knowledge, education, money or support. I have few friends and almost no confidence; I'm not sure anything will work out well . . ." Fear steps in and gets a grip, a tight grip on such people and any decision that might be made at this time is procrastinated. No action is taken and no results are achieved.

Here's a simple four-step idea and plan of action that will help you become the person you've always wanted to be. It's a formula designed to make all your dreams come true, allow you to become a happier person, have more money, have peace of mind and enjoy life to the fullest. Just promise yourself that you will utilize these four simple steps in everything you do. You just cannot find a reason or invent one on why you should not. Here is the multimillion dollar idea cheque for you to *use;* not just keep on file!

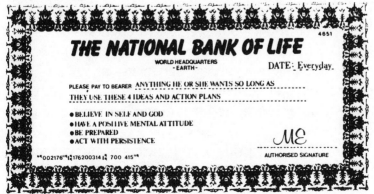

THE NATIONAL BANK OF LIFE

WORLD HEADQUARTERS
- EARTH -

4651

DATE: Everyday

PLEASE PAY TO BEARER ANYTHING HE OR SHE WANTS SO LONG AS

THEY USE THESE 4 IDEAS AND ACTION PLANS

- BELIEVE IN SELF AND GOD
- HAVE A POSITIVE MENTAL ATTITUDE
- BE PREPARED
- ACT WITH PERSISTENCE

ME

AUTHORISED SIGNATURE

⁕⁕002176⁕⁕⦂176200314⦂⁂ 700 415⁕⁕

1. Believe in Self and God

"What you sow, so shall you reap." If you plant watermelon seeds, you won't grow grapes but watermelons. The same is true of our thoughts. Our beliefs are conditioned by repeated exposure (programming). When we plant the thoughts of a poor self-image in our minds, these thoughts manifest themselves in our outer behavior. This is common in the majority of people because they do not believe in themselves or believe in God. If you knew that God is within you, would you dare to attempt *anything?* I believe you would.

You have all heard such familiar statements as, "God helps those who help themselves." "When you help yourself, then the God within works for you." "If God be with (within) us, who can be against us?" "God is everywhere!" If he is everywhere, he must be within you too. So there is no better place to search than *within yourself*—for the answers to your problems.

Remember, what others have done and are doing, you can do too, maybe even better. You possess the same God-given powers within yourself, ready to respond to your wishes. But, your future progress must be earned through your everyday thoughts and actions. If you try to meet the pressures of life by relying more and more upon liquor, drugs, sedatives, stimulants and devices outside yourselves, you will be getting further away from yourself, and from the *God* centre of your own being.

You are an offspring of your parents, your parents of your grandparents, they, in turn, of your great-grandparents. Ultimately we go back to one man and one woman in the beginning of time. Where did they come from? Since they were created "in the image of God," then by the natural law of cause and effect that same image and spark of God has been carried in every human being past, present and to come in the future too. That means that right now, you have the powers of *God* within you to use whenever you like.

With such enormous inner potential, human beings nevertheless go about their daily routine with no excitement on their faces and more excuses to give for nonachievement. Little wonder they achieve little and have no peace of mind!

The great achievers believe in themselves, in the God within and around them and, with that firm belief, attempt anything worthwhile without any fear. They deserve and get everything they sincerely desire for themselves, their loved ones and others also. Dr. Norman Vincent Peale, the greatest positive thinker of our generation, whom I respect and admire as my mentor, says that in working towards any goals in life, "first, pray (counsel with God) about it to make sure it is the right goal, for if it isn't the right goal, then it's a wrong thing to do and no wrong thing every turned out to be right."

When your God within tells you (through your feelings) that you are doing the right thing, believe it and go right on. Become aware of your actions and decisions to make sure they are not due to your previous mental programing. Sometimes things may turn out to be bad, or everything may go wrong. Maintain belief in God and go on. Your difficulties probably are happening to test you, to strengthen you and to prepare you for the great things that lie ahead for you. I know it's true, I always keep going on and I know that Almighty God never intended to hurt us in anyway.

When you planted some good seeds in your tilled garden did you do so anxiously wondering and worrying if they would every grow? Probably not; you actually believed they would grow. All you did was water the beds, pulled out the weeds that grew around the area, even though you could not see any sprouts for a few days or even weeks. Remember your excitement when the seeds actually sprouted and you could see those cute little shoots?

The same goes for our thoughts, the seeds planted in our mind. It's our choice whether to plant unhealthy or healthy and good thoughts. The results will be of the same breed. Holding positive, good and healthy thoughts in our minds is not an easy task; it's easier said than done. One of the main reasons is that we are (sad to say) constantly surrounded by negative people, ideas and news. It takes constant weeding to get rid of these negative influences and thoughts. We need to mix with and share positive ideas, thoughts and feelings with the same kind of people or people who want to learn. Read more books, listen to many cassettes and expose ourselves to seminars, programs, workshops, conventions and trainings in the positive, personal and mental health development areas.

These same thoughts (seeds) will grow sooner or later and they will manifest themselves in your actions and behaviours to make you the kind of person that you always wanted to be. The excitement of seeing yourself growing in the direction of your choice is inexplicable. You are the grand total of your thoughts. You are what you believe you are. If you are not happy with what's happening to you on the outside, take an honest inner look and remember what William James said, "Human beings can alter their lives by altering their attitudes of mind."

2. Have A Positive Mental Attitude

Should you break a leg in an accident, you might react in two ways. Cry, and blame the world or yourself for the stupid mistake. Become angry with yourself, knowing that you could have avoided the accident, become angry with others who could have stopped it from happening; scold them, scream at them and suffer in pain. On the other hand, you could also think positively, saying to yourself or others, "Thank God I still have my other leg to walk with, my hands are O.K. I'm still alive and well." In other words, what has happened has happened; accept it and go on from there. Make the best of what there is, instead of complaining and crying about your misfortune.

Having a positive mental attitude means counting our blessings instead of our problems. When the business fails, when you do not pass the examination or do not achieve whatever goal you have been working towards all these years, look at that failure as *temporary defeat* and ask yourself, "Since it has happened, what did I learn from that experience?" By doing that, you will discover many exciting things that you could improve or avoid in future and you will want to go on with greater determination and energy.

James Bond was trapped in a four-walled room by his archvillian and it looked like certain death for Bond, as the four walls began to move inwards, slowly threatening to crush 007. Not like him to give in so easily, he looked around the walls studying the area that was getting smaller and smaller. He noticed that there were two manholes on the ground. Without wasting any more time, he struggled with the first manhole and opened it. It was a septic tank emitting a strong, repulsive odor. The tank was full to the top and at one side it touched the marker which indicated "7 FEET." Bond, being just a little over six feet tall, knew that if he jumped in he would drown. He quickly opened the second manhole and discovered that this, too, was a septic tank with the same foul odor. But the level in this tank indicated "6 FEET." The walls were getting too close for comfort now. What did he do? What would *you* do if you were James Bond? Being in the worst possible situation imaginable, he is still optimistic as he tells himself, "Thank goodness I'm still alive!"

Did it ever occur to you that you could actually choose to be happy or sad, irrespective of what your situation might be? How you want to feel is within your power of choice at all times. Dr. Murray Banks, a wonderful humorous speaker and famous psychologist from New York, advocates adjusting mentally to the situations that occur in our lives. He calls it "mental adjustment" or what we would call a positive mental attitude. "Two women lose a sweetheart," he explains, "one commits suicide, the other adjusts to the situation by saying, 'So what, I'll find another!' and she goes out looking for another sweetheart knowing that this time she will find a better one." How do you adjust when everything you do fails? Do you give up and quit, or do you have faith in the God-given power within and keep on trying over and over, knowing and believing that it has to happen positively in your favor sooner or later? You make those choices.

3. Be Prepared

In one simple sentence, the formula is: *Do the ground-work!* One of the basic fundamentals in achieving anything worthwhile is creating a strong foundation and building your dreams on that base. The bigger or higher your goals, the deeper and more thorough is the foundation or research and study required. Ask any architect and he will tell you that in order to build a highrise building, the ground on which the structure is to be erected has to be tested, checked, analyzed; many soil tests carried out before the piling is begun. Steel bars are driven into the ground to make sure that the edifice stands on firm ground. The higher the tower, the deeper the pilework; the more work, time and money involved. At every phase of the tower erection, construction is periodically checked to make sure that the tower is built according to plan. The merest one-tenth of an inch off the mark can spell disaster! This building finally houses human beings and keeps them safe, happy and secure.

Our lives also need to be built in the same manner. The foundation has to be built if we are to rise higher in our careers. Our bodies must be maintained by good nutrition and exercise, just as the building has to be maintained too. Preparation for the examinations must be made by constant study, long before the time comes for sitting for the tests. Likewise, people cannot handle a position for which they have not prepared themselves. They must be prepared mentally, physically, emotionally, knowledgewise, socialwise and otherwise.

You may have noticed that the professional golfer, singer, runner, speaker, salesman, entertainer and all the other professionals prepare themselves long before they actually become winners and achievers. Having spoken to many winners, achievers and champions in the business, sports and sales worlds, I have found that these great people have actually put in hundreds to thousands of hours of training, practicing, rehearsing and sweating it out before they become winners. Let's follow their example too.

Anyone who wants good health, happiness, friends, growth, peace, security, freedom, leisure and all the opportunities ought to follow Zig Ziglar's very simple formula. Build the foundation of your life on the following pillars and you will have acquired all the above mentioned benefits. The pillars of success are the foundation stones for a richer life. Build into your life, HONESTY, LOYALTY, FAITH, CHARACTER and INTEGRITY, then cover it with the roof of LOVE. It will not be surprising to see you climb to the top!

Nothing beats preparing, planning and setting goals well in advance before you begin your journey in life. The founder of the Boy Scouts movement, Lord Baden

Powell understood the concept of "Be Prepared" and made it their motto. I'm sure they wouldn't mind if we borrowed that advice to use in our lives.

4. Act With Persistence

All the best ideas, techniques, methods and systems for achieving success and happiness are useless if you do not take action. As a matter of fact, a mediocre idea backed up with plenty of action will do more for you than the best idea which remains only a theory without action. Become an *action* oriented person. Become a *doer* rather than a talker. The world has progressed this far because of the dedicated few, the five percenters who went all out and did what they dreamed about, set goals and persisted relentlessly to make this world a better place in which to live.

What is your contribution towards the betterment of life, your family, your organization, your community, your country, and to humanity itself? Will you leave this world a better place and make people happier because *you* passed their way and made them better people? Will your contributions be useful for the future of your children and their generations to come? It does not have to be money you leave behind; it could be an idea, a product, a few kind words, a statement, maybe a memory that would last forever.

Inertia has killed more people both mentally and physically than those who toil day and night physically. Let's not be afraid of failing. The only way to find out if we are going to be successful in any project, undertaking or goal of our own choice is to *do it*. We may fail in the process. So what? Get up and get back to it again with increased zest and enthusiasm by learning from our mistakes. Every single step towards achievement, even a failure, gets you closer towards your goal. The main thing to remember is that it's not the number of times you fail, but the number of times you get back into action. One rule to follow is to try it just once more, each time you fail.

Thomas Edison, in my opinion, was the greatest persistent human being who ever lived. His determination to try once more led to over 1,000 attempts before he discovered the right filament for the light bulb! Had it not been for his persistence or had he stopped after 999 attempts, you and I would probably still be living in darkness today. The next time you feel like giving up, think of the effort and time Edison put into bringing brightness to the world and go for it . . . *try it one more time!*

Every time I watch our one-and-a-half-year-old son Navin, it reminds me of myself and the persistence I display in my life. Whenever he wants something, I test him by telling myself that if he keeps trying persistently to get whatever he wants for 30 to 40 times, I will give in if he exceeds that number. I always lose and I'm glad I do. It builds his confidence knowing that sooner or later he will get it. I believe that our children can teach us a lot of things which we have forgotten.

The woman you married, the mother of your children might be a perfect example of your persistence. Remember how, perhaps, she did not want to give you a second look? How she said "no" over and over again each time you wanted to date her? How you kept on persistently wooing her until little by little she became fond of you. Then, finally, when you asked her to marry you, she said, "Yes!" All the nos added up to become a yes. Similarly, with persistence, all your failures will add up to become the success you seek.

Now's The Right Time for Action

The belief in yourself has been confirmed. You know GOD is backing you up, your attitude is positive, your plans are set and the ground work is complete with the research done and the knowledge obtained. You are prepared! The only thing left to do is to *act now*, to put into action the plans and goals you set. Let no amount of discourgement, failures, obstacles or setbacks stop you from making your dreams come true. The journey could be rough but, why worry? You are prepared; and with your mental adjustment towards thinking positively, you are going to enjoy every moment of your trip through this world. There is no need to worry how things will work out later when you have done your best while you are here.

There need be no fear in making the return trip either. With God as your co-pilot, making the trip together will make you happy, knowing you are in good hands. After all, if "God be with us, who dares to be against us?"

GINGER BONDI

Quest for Excellence
2612 Judith Street
Metairie, LA 70003
(New Orleans area)
(504) 454-0025

Ginger Bondi

Ginger Bondi is a successful businesswoman, entrepreneur, and an ex-corporate executive of two major international companies. She has taught her skills of sales, management, training and organizational development to countless achievers. Winner of many top awards for outstanding performance in sales and management, she speaks with the authority of experience.

She is the author of two books and cassette tape series available through her consulting firm, "Quest For Excellence," dedicated to releasing the potential power in people. As a professional development specialist, Ginger Bondi has inspired audiences with uplifting, humorous illustrations delivered in an animated and enthusiastic style. Using a many faceted approach to a variety of topics, she lends a refreshing slant to growth, development and achievement. A diversified background with over 20 years of extensive study, training and experience in these areas, qualifies her to speak about such interrelated subjects as Success Consciousness; Motivation; Sales/Marketing/ Management; Quality Service Power; Time Organization, Communications and Human Relations.

An earlier career as an interior designer allows her also to offer Interior Decorating as a speaking topic. She focuses on strategies and specific "How-To's." Ginger is a member of the National Speakers Association, International Platform Association, Toastmasters International, American Society For Training and Development, and a certified consultant for Performax Systems International (leaders in the field of behavioral sciences).

GET OFF YOUR LAUNCHING PAD

By Ginger Bondi

"Do not follow where the path may lead—go, instead, where there is no path . . . and leave a trail!"

—Anonymous

Equipment Inspection and Instrument Check

Before any launching, officials conduct tests to verify operational efficiency. All equipment is tested and instruments checked. As we go through our journey of life, we, too, should inspect the equipment of the vehicle in which we travel . . . our mind and body. The instruments we use are: (1) our emotional and mental attitudes; (2) our methods of thinking; (3) our behavioral habits. It's important to keep a constant check on these instruments because they not only determine the course we will follow, but will guide and steer us all the way. If we do not have the gauges on these instruments set properly, we not only won't end up where we wanted to go—we won't even enjoy the trip.

We must beware of one treacherous element that will clog up the whole works. It's called procrastination. You will do well to heed the warning signals. Putting off reaching for your dreams or attempting to accomplish the goals you'd like for your life is most often caused by various fears . . . the most common one being fear of failure. Fear of failure puts sludge on your confidence which will create a murky build-up of procrastination. Procrastination is a stubborn obstruction that will hinder your life and bog down your hope of accomplishment. A continued habit of procrastination will decay your dreams. All the hope of your life will turn to dust before you do. So, the very first inspection of your equipment should be a check to see if procrastination is jamming up any of your instruments. Let me tell you how mine finally got checked.

A few years ago, I heard a speaker make the statement that it sometimes takes death to teach us about life. I didn't really understand that statement until recently. In the fall of 1978, shortly after giving me away at a beautiful wedding to my present husband, my father began to show signs of failing health. Though he had never been sick before, his symptoms began to impair his functioning. He was in and out of the hospital frequently, requiring my mother, my aunt and me to alternate shifts staying with him.

Watching him decline from a robust, strapping tower of strength (who resembled a football player), to an uncontrolled state of weakness was not only degrading and humiliating to him; it was heartbreaking for me. I had faced adversities before—I'd been through three major surgeries at an early age, a long and tormenting destruction of my first marriage, a severe automobile accident, serious financial problems and many other onerous experiences. But, the death of my father was the most grevious cross I had yet to bear.

Only twelve weeks later, my mother was required to have surgery. While still in the throes of grief over the loss of my father, I was given the news that she had an advanced cancer with little hope of survival. Ironically, after surgery, she was placed in a room directly across the hall from the one my father had last occupied. I was having quite a struggle with my emotions, but every time I left her room to let them escape for a while, I was forced to face squarely into the room in which my father had died so recently . . . creating a cruel reminder of what had just passed and a simultaneous amplification of what was to come. Following surgery, my mother's suffering was to extend over nineteen and a half months of the most potent and frequent chemotherapy treatments prescribed which were just as horrendous, if not worse, than the disease itself.

Throughout that time, I was to witness and share what must be the most extreme physical and emotional agonies to which a human being can be subjected. Surely, the struggle and suffering were worse for my parents, but those three and one-half years were absolutely the most devastating period of my life. My parents gave me much and taught me much throughout my life—but, through their dying periods, they taught me more about life and living than ever before. Dealing with someone close to you dying on a daily basis for over three and one-half years, brings your own mortality into sharp focus.

As I tended to my parents, the reality of our mortality loomed before me as an ever-growing giant. It was no longer an abstract event far into the future that never seemed to ring true as a reality which would definitely happen. I began to develop an awareness and desire to make better use of my time and my life. I thought of all the things I'd wanted to do and didn't. I thought of all the wasted time . . . all the opportunities missed or not followed through . . . all the cards and letters never sent . . . the phone calls never made—all the kind words and love unshared because of the habit of putting things off. "Oh, for the touch of the vanished hand, and the sound of the voice that is still!" (Tennyson).

Why do we put things off? Especially those things that are important to ourselves and others we care about? Procrastination is a malady of epidemic proportions. My habit of procrastination was being chipped away day after day over those three and a half years, but it was so deeply imbedded, only the surface had been scratched. Usually, my mother was very stoic and her inner feelings were kept hidden. But, about two weeks before she died, my mother became very emotional—and began to express the overwhelming struggle she was having.

Through great tears streaming down her face, she said, "I'm not afraid to die, but it's so *hard* . . . it's so hard to give up on all the things I'll never do or see. I know I've had more time than some people, but it wasn't enough. I never really did all I wanted to do. I don't have much to show for my life!" She cried for quite a while longer, then she added, "I didn't do anything meaningful except raise my children. I wish I had done more . . . I still want to do more . . . but, I'll never get out of this bed again; and very soon, I'll just be gone from this world—now, it's too late!"

Aside from my feeling of helplessness and intense emotional feelings for her, at that very moment something exploded inside of me that blasted away every trace of procrastination and in it's place a sense of urgency began to swell. As the days and weeks passed, that sense of urgency continued to build momentum at an ever-increasing rate until it reached proportions that could no longer be contained within my body. It began reaching out beyond myself.

I started noticing other people who seemed less than content with where they were in their life. I became more aware of the importance of statistics such as 85% of the population working in jobs they don't like every day of their lives; 95% of people living only mediocre lives with the hopes and dreams of their youth shattered and half forgotten. Others, who haven't forgotten their dreams are submersed in frustration or bitterness. I wondered how many of them truly realize that they could do something about it—or what the consequences are if they don't! I wanted to shout the message to everyone I saw who seemed to be "just existing." My mother's phrase, "I didn't do anything meaningful . . . and now it's too late!" kept ringing in my ears. I, too, wanted to do something meaningful. I always had. Now, not only for myself but I wanted to make a contribution to others. I wanted to help them get *more* out of their lives if there was any way possible I could do that. I wanted to make them realize, time waits for no man.

As far back as I can remember, I wanted to be an author and a speaker. But, I always procrastinated. I didn't think I had anything really important to say. At least, nothing that hadn't been said before by those more qualified than I. What credentials did I have to make statements regarding people's lives? Then I remembered my father's attitude. Whatever you do, no matter how menial the task, if you always strive for excellence, it will be worth doing. If you make yourself a quality person, everything you do will reflect the highest quality. Now, you don't need an extensive education or superior financial background to make yourself a quality person. It doesn't matter what your past was like, you can make yourself and your future whatever you want.

My father grew up in very hard circumstances and never completed high school, but he constantly strove to excel. Throughout his career, he was highly regarded by his peers as well as his superiors for the quality of his work and his personal integrity. He experienced many periods of what seemed to be defeat. But, he picked himself up each time with an urge toward greater effort to try harder. He continued to rise until he achieved the position of his goal. But he had a desire to succeed in a business of his own. After one attempt that ended in failure, he determined to try again and succeeded beyond his expectations. I praise the Lord for seeing the expression of pride and joy on his face that all winners wear when victory comes.

How I wish he could see the published pages I've written and the audiences who applaud my presentations. How I wish he could meet the people who've thanked me for touching their lives in a positive way and know that he was my role model. How I wish my mother could know that she did, in fact, do something meaningful by creating the sense of urgency within me, not only to make something of my life, but to make a contribution towards helping others to succeed also. Hopefully, multitudes of people will read her message that I'm sharing and be moved to profit by it. I am dedicating this chapter to her and the courageous battle she fought to sustain her life. If I can move but one person to break out of mediocrity and seek their full potential, it will be to her credit. She created an avalanche of reality that came crashing down on me in an overwhelming rush to focus on fulfillment. Life, as well as success, is an adventurous journey of perpetual seeking, searching and pursuit. Each and every day counts. *Now* is the time to chart your course.

Charting Your Course

If you are plagued by procrastination, let me give you at least one good reason to conquer it: *You, too, have a limited time to live!* Does that statement shock you or surprise you? It shouldn't. It is an inescapable fact that cannot be denied. Does it serve any purpose for us to try to deny it, simply because we do not know the length of time? Is it in our best interest to evade the issue or to pretend not to be aware of it? Why do we put off doing what we really want to do with our lives until an undetermined "someday," or until "after" a certain period or event takes place? How many times have you heard, "after" the kids are grown, "after" the bills are paid off, "after" I retire, etc.?

Over 95% of the time, another "after" develops as each one is passed. Society, in general, has become so entrapped by the habit of procrastination, it has begun to accept putting things off as a *modus operandi.* There is nothing sadder in life (or more final) than someone who "could have been" or "was going to do." What makes you think you have a guarantee of a nebulous "someday"? Death is no respecter of age . . . it takes 2-year-olds, 18, 28, 40, and 50-year-olds, as well as 80-year-olds. It has a message—and that message is, *"The Time to Live Is Now!"* There is no second chance.

Life is a precious gift. We shouldn't squander it, or treat it disrespectfully, or, worse, take it for granted. It is meant to be lived to the *fullest potential.* Most of us don't have any idea when our lives will end—it could be many years from now, or it could be moments from now. Let's just suppose for our purposes that you did know . . . and, let's further suppose that it isn't a great length of time, but reasonable. How many things (that are presently in your life) would become unimportant?

Think about it. What would you eliminate to get the most effective use of the time you have to live? What would become your priorities? What is it that you would most want to do? What accomplishments or achievements would be most desirable to you? *Why Aren't*

You Doing That Now? Why? Now is the time to chart *your* course. The answers to the questions just asked should be your goals. If you didn't answer them, take the time now to do it, answering each one on separate sheets of paper. Many of us spend half our time wishing for things we could have if we didn't spend half our time wishing. At the time of graduation, one class of Yale University seniors was asked if they had written any specific financial goals. Ten percent of the seniors had specific goals, but had not written them. Three percent had put their specific goals on paper. The rest had no specific goals. When they were surveyed twenty years later, the 3% had out-performed the other 97% combined! Having written goals allows you to read them regularly to re-energize your motivation and action.

There is a story about a man who noticed indications of superior marksmanship in many areas throughout a small town. On trees, barns and fences all over town, were bullet holes in the exact center of the targets. When he asked to meet the expert shot, it turned out to be the village idiot. Amazed, the man asked, "How in the world did you do it?" "Easy as pie," came the answer, "I shoot first, and draw the circles afterward!" A great majority of people plan their lives this way—never going after what they really want; just resigning themselves to settle for whatever they get.

Once you've written your goals, stay focused on them by visualizing yourself as having achieved them. It is important to imagine a clear picture of yourself in great detail as already having attained and possessing what-ever it is that you desire. The subconscious mind accepts this as reality and begins to set forces in motion to bring it about. Also, use affirmations to yourself, saying that you *can* and *will* do it. These positive statements to yourself will reinforce your confidence, eradicate any doubts, and replace self-defeating negative thoughts. Visualize it, affirm it, believe it . . . and it will manifest itself! If you'll stretch your mind and your vision, your horizons will expand also. You must believe it before you can achieve it; and "seeing is believing." That belief will be your propellent.

The Fuel

We must have the proper fuel to take us where we want to go in life. William James confirms, "It is our belief at the beginning of a difficult undertaking which will determine its successful outcome." Every good ambition or desire in your heart is a whisper from God telling you that the ability to attain it is within you. Achieving your aspirations involves work, but hard work alone is not enough to bring success The world is full of people who work hard, but have little to show for it.

It is creative thinking and a firm belief in your ability to execute your ideas that will propel you to rise above the commonplace. "According to your faith be it unto you." (Matt. 9:29, KJV). Let me give you an example of the power within that statement from my own experience. In the 1960's I had an automobile accident which caused major injuries. There was damage to my central nervous system which caused partial paralysis (the entire left side of my body was affected).

The pain was so severe, that it could not be relieved even with the maximum dosage of morphine. My body reacted to the extreme burden of pain with a minor stroke, distorting the left side of my face. As a last resort, I was packed in ice to freeze the affected areas, which was an ordeal in itself. Though I could hardly stand to be touched or moved, I was also put into a traction apparatus which had to be disconnected and reconnected at regular intervals as the ice melted and called for changing me and the bed clothes.

I was told that I would never regain full use of my left side without intricate surgery. However, one of the risks of the surgery was the possibility of *total* paralysis! I was not willing to take that risk, but all I could think about was that I wanted to return to normal functioning. I had a great amount of faith and decided that my fate was not for any man to decide; it was God's decision. I felt strongly that God did not intend for me to remain that way, but perhaps, He was testing my faith.

I had a family medical book which showed the various nerves and networks of connections throughout the body. I used this to start concentrating and visualizing power and energy being sent by my brain throughout these networks to the affected parts with commandments for these nonfunctioning areas to move. I truly believed it would work and never allowed doubts to enter my mind. I did this constantly as I laid there day after day trying to lift and move my left arm and leg and straighten the left side of my face.

Ever so slowly, as I worked on it and prayed, the parts

began to move. At first, it was hardly a noticeable change. I continued to visualize myself as back to normal—not only walking and functioning, but even dancing delightedly to happy music. Gradually, I got bigger results. Inch by inch over a period of many months, I got back on my feet. I reached a point where I could go to physical therapy with a little help. Though it was still painful, I went daily. While I continued to exercise, my faith in God and myself grew stronger as I progressed. I experienced the God-given power of the mind in a way that brought the scriptures to life for me. "All things are possible to him that believeth." (Mark 9:23, KJV).

Today, there are only a few movements which I cannot maneuver well, and, for the most part, people never detect them. Have faith—and the Lord will always carry you through. Aren't we blessed to have the opportunity to start anew each day? When you arise in the morning, rejoice in the day that has been given to you. Be thankful to be alive, well and functional. Be grateful that you have a powerful mind to use for any purpose that you choose. Recognize that you do have choices. Choose exactly what you want your life to be from this day forward . . . and it will be yours if you just believe it can be. Isn't that exciting? Emerson put it more profoundly when he said, "What lies behind us and what lies before us are tiny matters compared to what lies within us."

The Power

Besides fuel, the vehicle and the operator must have

power. You have a *will* and it gives you the power to *control* your thinking habits, attitudes, and reactions. Exercising this power is vital to success. We are what we are and where we are because of our habitual thinking. "As a man thinketh, so is he." Control of the mind is not difficult, but you must make a conscious effort to acheive it and be persistent. The subconscious mind is influenced more strongly and acts more readily on thoughts that are well mixed with emotion. The most effective results will come from thoughts mixed with the emotions of faith, desire and enthusiastic persistence.

If you fail to plant positive thoughts supported by positive emotions, the subconscious mind will feed upon whatever reaches it as a result of your neglect. Since our thoughts and our will are the only things in this life over which we have complete control, I'm sure you can readily see that you do have the ability to "shut-out" any negative thinking (if you really want to). Napoleon Hill said, "The mind attracts to one the exact equivalent of that which one thinks about most often." This is called the Law of Attraction.

Thoughts are powerful forces. Every great accomplishment in history, every invention, all the progress in the world today first began as a thought. (And so did every war!) So, be careful of what you think about, because you're going to get it. Positive and negative thoughts and emotions cannot occupy the mind at the same time; the choice is yours. Be alert to negative thoughts and emotions (such as fear, anger and revenge), and immediately reject and replace them with positive, affirmative thoughts mixed with positive emotions.

Your habits of thought also create your attitude. It is safe to say that attitude is everything in life. It has been said that your "altitude in life will be determined by your attitude in life." You actually create your own environment and the way you perceive it by your attitude (which is a direct result of your thinking habits). William James said, "The greatest discovery of my generation is that people can alter their lives by altering their attitudes of mind." It is worth mentioning here also, that our attitude is projected to others and this factor has much to do with the quality of our life. Recognize that your psychological and emotional attitude shows in your facial expressions, your gestures, your tone of voice, and even in your posture and carriage. If you don't get the right attitude from others, consider the undeniable fact that people usually reflect the attitude that you give them. "As ye sow, so shall ye reap."

When you encounter someone with a poor attitude who treats you badly, exercise your right to maintain a good attitude. It costs you nothing to reach out and give them what they so desperately need . . . caring, understanding, assurance, or recognition. Say something nice to them or find something about which you can sincerely compliment them. Help them to feel good about themselves—*give*—and watch what happens. Everyone responds to praise and appreciation. People will flock to a person who helps them think more highly of themselves. Realize that another person's anger, or other bad emotion, is their choice of attitude and their problem. If you react in a similar manner, you have just stolen another person's problem and there is no value in it! Franklin Jones warns, "Be careful of sharp words, you may have to eat them!"

Keys to the Switch

Taking action is the key that will turn the "switch" from dream to reality. *Do whatever you have to do.* Stop worrying about holding on to what you've got, and go after what you really want. Many wait for time and circumstances to be just right before they start something worthwhile. Well, time and circumstances will never be "just right." Start where you are now and work with whatever you have at your command. You can always increase your resources and improve as you go along. If what you can do now is only 50% as good as it can be, that's still 100% better than nothing. To be prepared when bigger opportunities knock, seek specialized knowledge relative to your endeavor. Learn everything you can about your field of interest from every source available. Ben Franklin wisely stated, "If a man empties his purse into his head, no man can take it away from him." There are special courses, books, tapes, and seminars covering virtually every field. "Where there is a will, there is a way."

Education is not sufficient unto itself for earning a good living—education is knowing *what to do* with your learning after you have it! We can control the conditions that cause us to rise to the top or remain at the bottom depending on our desire and the habits we choose to acquire. Always be willing to *do* more. Practice more to be the best you can be. You don't have to be better than others in your field; just willing to do more. The champions of the world are those who keep on going at the point that others would quit. The amateur always has an excuse—the pro is his own worst critic. Winners do the ordinary things an extraordinary number of times. That's what sets them apart from the rest. Nothing develops character like discipline. You must be your own task master. "Reputation is what you're supposed to be; character is what you are. Real character is what you are when nobody's looking." It doesn't matter who signs your paycheck; you must remember that you are working for *yourself*. Successful people are those who are willing to do the things failures will not!

Fire the Engines

Enthusiasm is the spark that will ignite the fire in your engines with excitement, vitality and energy. The best example of enthusiasm is in the spirit of a child— fascinated by everything and enjoying life to the fullest. Emerson said, "Nothing great was ever achieved without enthusiasm." The word enthusiasm, from the Greek *entheos*, means *God in you* or *full of God*. That seems to verify that enthusiasm has the power to work miracles. It can be *both* cause and effect because it is contagious. It is one element that will induce others to join forces with you without persuasion. Enthusiasm announces to the world that you love life and people; that you have an awareness of the wonder and beauty in even the simplest things.

When you have this kind of zest for life, you develop the type of charisma that sparkles with "pizzazz"! If your life and your potential are suffering from apathy, you can take an interest in deliberately making yourself enthusiastic. "A merry heart doeth good like a medicine, but a broken spirit drieth the bones." (Prov. 17:22 KJV). Now, the emotions are not always subject to reason, but they are subject to action. Apply the *"as if"* principle. William James counsels, "If you want a quality, act *as if* you already had it." Shakespeare told us in Hamlet, "Assume a virtue if you have it not." We become what we act. Look at the best side of things. Stop dwelling on what you don't have and start thinking of what you do have. Don't waste energy on gripes and complaints; concentrate on what's good and what you can do with it. (If you don't think *every* day is great, try missing a few!) Approach everything you do with "gusto." The more you practice it, the sooner it will become an automatic habit to lift your spirits.

To fire your enthusiasm to it's highest degree, you may have to make some changes. A thorough self-appraisal must be made to determine what changes need to be made. This is a challenge. It's hard to improve ourselves—we're always finding somebody else who needs our attention more. But, when a man begins to learn the truth about himself, it frequently retards his program for reforming others. Among all new challenges, the reconstruction of self can be the greatest because when you change you (the real inner you), your entire life will literally begin to change simultaneously.

Many people today are miserable due mainly to an inferiority complex. Of course, this sets up a barrier to any accomplishment. We must realize what our problems are before we can come up with viable solutions. We must try to determine the reasons we have these inadequate emotional feelings. It can be a result of your own negative thinking which constantly reinforces a low self-image. You may feel a limited education or a poor social background has inhibited you. You may have accepted negative attitudes or opinions of other people toward you in your past experiences which have damaged your self-esteem. Perhaps, criticism from parents, teachers, or your peer groups has stayed with you. It may be that emphasis on previous mistakes or failures has become dominant in your thinking.

Any combination of the above reasons can cause you to maintain a low self-image and block the attainment of self-confidence and achievement. Regardless of what the reasons are, you have the ability to create a healthy self-image by consciously choosing to reverse these attitudes, thought patterns and feelings. I'm going to suggest certain steps you can take to develop a healthy self-confidence in addition to the processes already mentioned under the previous headings. A good way to start is by listing any and all of your previous successes.

Include any past undertaking which you concluded satisfactorily . . . no matter how incidental it may seem. Think back, and don't leave anything out. Next, identify all your talents, abilities and skills. Be generous with yourself—list everything you seem to have a flair for—don't overlook any knack you have. Take your time and don't stop too quickly. These are all your assets. Writing out a complete inventory of them will allow you to read them regularly (and add to them) as an important step in overcoming feelings of inadequacy and increasing confidence. As you study them, you will also become more aware of your potentials. "All the best work is done the way ants do things—by tiny, but untiring and regular additions." (Lafcadio Hearn)

All Systems On Go

Once all our "systems" are on go, we must develop the kind of determination and perseverance that refuses to be turned off, much less (heaven forbid) stopped. On our journey to success, we may encounter obstacles or setbacks. Obstacles are those terrifying things we see when we take our eyes off our goals. Setbacks are temporary delays or detours on our course. If we have firmly set our minds to go after our desires and goals, the seeds of success have been planted. Let us take our example for nuturing those seeds from nature. When seeds are planted in soil, roots and sprouts soon appear. As they reach for light and moisture, obstacles mean nothing to them. They will push small stones aside, go through wood, or extend themselves to grow around them. They are determined to emerge and produce fruit, vegetables, or flowers.

This kind of undefeatable spirit is illustrated in a story about Thomas Edison told by his son, Charles. In December of 1914, the great Edison industries were virtually destroyed by fire. Thomas Edison lost two million dollars that night and much of his life's work went up in smoke. Searching frantically for Thomas, his son found him standing near the fire . . . his face ruddy in the glow, his white hair blown in the December winds. Charles reports, "My heart ached for him. He was sixty-seven—no longer a young man—and everything was going up in flames." The next morning, as he walked about the charred embers of his hopes and dreams, Thomas Edison said, "There is great value in disaster. All our mistakes are burned up. Thank God, we can start anew." Three weeks after the fire, his firm delivered the first phonograph to the world. *Such is the spirit of determination and perserverance!* "Go, and do thou likewise."

Countdown

If you have ever watched the launching of any rockets, you probably noticed many people present. Many who made contributions to the completion of the project were not present, but it is obvious that it took the coordination and cooperation of countless people for the successful completion of the project . . . each contributing his or her own special skill, ability and talent. So, it is with you and your project. It is not possible for one individual to be an expert in all areas. Keeping this illustration in mind, your success will come much easier and faster if you will seek to associate with people who are already successful in your field. "Birds of a feather flock together." Ask for help—and heed their advice. Most are not only willing to help, but are usually flattered at the personal confidence in them which you are demonstrating by the asking. Attending conventions and conferences in your field of interest serves this purpose very well. But, a word of caution: choose carefully which "birds" you "flock" with—stay focused on your goal and remember why you're there. Keep in mind, if you want to soar with the eagles, you have to hang around with the eagles . . . but, if you hoot with the owls at night, you can't soar with eagles in the morning!

Lift Off

To make it easier to lift off your launching pad, lighten up! Transcend any obstacles with a sense of humor. Remember, success is a journey, not a destination. The rewards and satisfactions come more from the enjoyment of the trip than the achievement. Rise above majoring in the minors—in other words, "Don't sweat the small stuff!" Laughter, fun, playfulness and merriment add *joy* to life. Learn to laugh at yourself—don't take yourself too seriously. Make friends with yourself first—*relax and enjoy*. It doesn't cramp your style, it adds to your charm. (Charm is the ability to make someone else feel that both of you are wonderful!) That certain something that sets special people apart comes from within—from special feelings they have acquired. A part of those feelings is that they are comfortable with who they are and what they are. They value themselves, which gives them confidence and a sense of well-being . . . But, they don't take themselves too seriously! "Imagination was given to man to compensate him for what he is not; and a sense of humor was provided to console him for what he is."

Learn to *accept* your limitations, shortcomings, mistakes and failures without passing final judgement. Regard them as an indication of your ongoing progress in learning and *becoming*. We must *allow* ourselves to be a fallible human before we can befriend ourselves and get better in whatever areas we desire to improve. With affection and a sense of humor, we can help others learn the same things, too. Not only that, but a sense of humor can "de-fuse" tensions, aid healing and add years to your life . . . or, more importantly, add life to your years!

Enjoy your flight and make it a great trip!

"The winds and waves are always on the side
of the ablest navigators."

—Edward Gibbon

THOMAS W. FARANDA

Faranda & Associates
8680 Black Maple Drive
Eden Prairie, MN 55344
(612) 941-6242

Thomas W. Faranda

Tom Faranda is a management consultant, seminar presentor and author. He has presented his management development programs to business firms, government organizations, professional associations and medical operations in Canada, Australia, Alaska and in the continental United States.

In addition to earning an M.B.A. degree in international business and management, Tom holds a B.S. degree in the field of marketing and advertising. To broaden himself, he has also completed a Ph.D. degree program in education.

Tom is the author of several business articles and he has published a specialized management book which is utilized in Canada and the United States by code administrators.

Tom Faranda has held management positions in sales, product management, administration, marketing and health care. His varied experiences have provided him an insight into human and management problems, and have aided his ability to be a popular and effective presentor to people in all fields. He is on the Board of Directors of the Minnesota Chapter of the National Speakers Association.

This chapter is dedicated to

FRANK FAIETA

whose warm heart and generous spirit
touched so many of us.

SENSORY MOTIVATION
Using Your Senses To Break Through To Others
by thomas w. faranda

RULE OF SENSORY MOTIVATION

"Common sense, (which in truth is very uncommon) is the best sense I know of!"
—**Lord Chesterfield**

Sight, hearing, taste, touch and smell. All of these human senses are direct motivators to which we all relate. Use them well and you will notice a positive increase in how other people respond to you.

THE SENSE OF SIGHT

"There's none so blind as those who will not see . . ."
—**Jonathan Swift**

Of all human senses, the sense of sight has the strongest motivational impact on people. It is a sense that conveys messages without words, allows intense interaction between individuals and promotes the concept of self-motivation.

We use the phrase "eye contact" to represent the use of the sense of sight between people. Eye contact provides significant motivation to others because it adds value and self-worth to the receiver while demonstrating sincerity and credibility to the sender. Here's how it works:

When you meet another person's eyes, you are sending a message that says, "You are important. I want to look at you and share your thoughts and feelings. I care about you. You are worth a great deal to me." This visual interaction encourages people to upgrade their feelings about themselves. Eye contact upgrades their personal self-concept which in turn projects their worth to others. People with strong feelings of personal worth tend to be self-motivated people.

All of these complex feelings and interactions are communicated instantly and intensely without the need for additional communication or use of other human senses.

Non-Value Messages

When a person is unable to establish eye contact, an opposite effect occurs. Instead of adding value to others, value is taken away. The message is interpreted to mean, "I do not wish to look at you or know how you feel because you are not important to me." This message reduces the person's self-concept and damages the credibility of the person sending it. The resulting disappointment or anger of the person receiving the message negates any opportunity for effective inter-action and motivation.

Reserved or self-conscious people have great difficulty with eye contact. They tend to send out "non-value messages" without meaning to do so. Often, they cannot understand why people react to them in an ambivalent or negative manner. They frequently experience difficulty in helping others to motivate them-selves. This is so easily corrected. *Look* at people. Start sending positive "value messages."

Value Added

Think of the cause and effect relationship between eye contact, the use of the sense of sight and human motivation. Think of the messages that are being com-municated silently. This is why so many leaders are so effective in helping others to become motivated. They add value to other people by helping them perceive their own sense of worth. Effective sensory motivators always concentrate on "adding to" and not on "taking away."

Strategy of Observation

Observation is another facet of the use of the sense of sight. As Sherlock Holmes frequently commented to Dr. Watson, "You see, but you do not observe."

Much of the time we can tell a great deal about how people feel by simply observing how they act. The principle of "non-verbal communication" is based on this idea. Non-verbal communication is an *implicit* form of communication in which feelings, attitudes and concerns are "suggested" but not necessarily expressed. These "clues and cues from others" are critical indicators in helping others to be motivated.

The use of sight as a motivator is demonstrated in many ways. Who has the nicest office or the office closest to the boss? The position may not be discussed, but it is noticed. Actually, this practice was a basic motivation principle of the ancient Japanese feudal lords—the "daimyo's." They always made sure that their best samurai warriors were given homes closest to their own. It was a form of recognition through observation— an implicit motivator in an implicit society.

Nothing is more valuable to a motivator than the proper use of the sense of sight. Learn to use it well. You will surround yourself with people who are motivated because they feel good about themselves and about you.

> *"Those who bring sunshine to the lives of others cannot keep it from themselves."*
> **—James Barrie**

THE SENSE OF HEARING

> *"A wise old owl sat in an oak.*
> *The more he saw the less he spoke.*
> *The less he spoke the more he heard.*
> *Why can't we be like this wise old bird?"*
> **—Anonymous, 1875**

When researchers tested the people of the Maaban tribe of Africa, from the southern Sudan, they were amazed to find that these people could hear a whisper at a range of one hundred yards! These people had trained themselves to *hear!* Wouldn't it be wonderful if all of us would train ourselves to truly hear? We should really try to hear what others are saying to us, to "hear" their feelings and emotions and the messages they are trying to convey to us. When we really try to hear others, we are using the sense of hearing as part of the sensory motivation process.

This is a world filled with "sensory overload." To compensate, we tend to hear only that which we want to hear. This process is called selective perception—the programming of our minds and our hearing to pick up only the items in which we are particularly interested. Selective perception explains why *after* we buy a car, we hear more advertisements for that car than we did before we purchased it. Our mind has been programmed to "hear" anything which relates to our new vehicle.

People also employ selective perception to hear what they want to hear from others. It therefore becomes our personal and professional responsibility to send out clear signals that cannot be misunderstood. We must send a signal that motivates others to program their minds to "hear" our message. St. Paul, in his letter to th Corinthians in the Bible, said:

"If the trumpet give an uncertain sound,
who shall prepare for battle?"

To expect to hear, we must send messages that demand to be heard. Messages that are expressed correctly. Messages that are consistent verbally and non-verbally. If we expect others to hear *us*, we must be willing to hear *them*.

This is a society which rewards us too much for talking and not enough for listening. People universally value others they perceive as "good listeners." Certainly there must be a sound reason for the old saying: "God gave us two ears and only one mouth. Maybe He was trying to tell us something!" It is the listening process, you see, that is so essential to a sensory motivator.

A sensory motivator listens to people because listening sends out the message that they are important. Their words have value. We help people to motivate themselves by helping them to understand and accept the power of positive personal self-worth.

Most of us have probably shared the experience of having our boss ask our opinion and then listen to us. If the request was sincere, we responded in a manner that was motivated as well as informational. If we felt the request was insincere, however, we felt abused and were demotivated.

This feeling comes from our childhood. As children all of us wanted our parents to listen to us. We craved their attention. We went out of our way to promote a response. We "listened" for their reactions toward our actions. We wanted to be heard!

In many ways we are all still children. We want to be heard. When we are heard we feel better. We want someone to listen. We feel motivated when they respond with genuine interest. The entire concept of the Japanese "quality circles" is based on this same premise. People will be motivated when someone listens to their ideas. This listening skill, however, is not limited to any one group of people. It is a universal truth in the generic family of man!

The listening process provides us with the strength of inner motivation which is based on positive value messages. When we teach ourselves to hear, to really listen to the feelings and messages of others, we teach ourselves to be effective sensory motivators.

THE SENSE OF TASTE

"He that is great among you shall be your servant."
—Jesus
"To lead the people, walk behind them."
Lao-Tzu

Taste is considered by many people to be a useless sensory motivator. They feel that the sense of taste just does not fit into the concept of motivation. Golda Meir, former Premier of Israel, would not agree. She was famous for bringing world leaders to her kitchen table and serving them home baked delights before their serious discussions of world events and problems.

Throughout history, people of all nationalities have always stressed the significance of "breaking bread together." The great leaders of the world, regardless of nationality or religion, have stressed the importance of serving the people. Mahatma Gandhi of India practiced the humbling art of serving people from all walks of life.

We remember our mothers baking cookies and serving them to us—another example of the connection between taste, serving and motivation. Have you ever had the experience of having your boss serve *you* coffee? It is a motivator's way of sending the same "value messages" we have been discussing. In this case, the message is the same: "I serve you because I respect you. You have value in my eyes." The significance is in serving other people. This is especially effective when performed by a person of higher position for a person of lower position.

The use of the sense of taste, with its inherent value messages in the act of serving others, is definitely a positive aspect of sensory motivation. Work at discovering meaningful ways to implement this tool in your system of sensory motivation.

THE SENSE OF TOUCH

"Reach out and touch someone . . ."
—N.W. Bell Telephone Co.

In our music, our interpersonal relationships and our society, we are all crying out to be touched. Our world has a continually higher population density, yet we often find ourself increasingly isolated from others and from the warm and human response generated by the sense of touch.

Touch must be a part of every person's life every day. When we need support we yearn to reach out and touch those who are closest to us. We need to feel we *can* reach out for this support and caring without indicating weakness in our character or inability to control our lives. From childhood we learn the value and wonder of touching. As adults, however, too many of us retreat into isolation. We try to live up to the code of macho foolishness which says we must handle everything by ourselves. "No man is an island," wrote John Donne in his *Devotions*. How right he was in his assessment of the human need for loved ones and the human longing for touch.

Touching is a sensory motivator because it helps to break down barriers between people. Americans require "personal space barrier" of about three feet all around us, according to statistics. This is our way of isolating ourselves from others. Only close friends or loved ones are allowed within the three-foot space.

We need to reduce our personal space requirements. We must reach out more often to make the human contacts that break the barriers that isolate us. When we take that risk, we send an important human message: "I want to know you. You seem to be a good person. You are important." These are the "value messages" from which both parties emerge a little larger, a little better, a little less self-centered.

For centuries the handshake has been used to assist us in breaking space barriers. Once you have physically touched someone, your personal space distance is reduced. You have the opportunity for more interaction and a stronger relationship. Men and women should both make a concerted effort to utilize the handshake as a means to a better end.

Using touch as a sensory motivator must be more than a mere physical act. To truly "reach out and touch someone," you should touch them physically, emotionally, and spiritually. This holistic approach stresses that each of us is influenced by mind, body and spirit. These are the three aspects of our individuality which are inseparable when considering the holistic person.

In the practice of holistic medicine, physicians are taught to look at the total person, not just to treat the physical symptoms. We must learn to consider the total person—the complex of physical, emotional and spiritual considerations which make each person a unique and special individual. We cannot begin to understand or use touch as a sensory motivator until we accept the holistic concept, and master the value messages concept inherent in the touching process.

THE SENSE OF SMELL

"If thou hast a loaf of bread, sell half and buy flowers. For bread nourisheth the body, but flowers the soul."
—Prophet Mohammad

We use our sense of smell very little in our society as a sensory motivator. We focus on the importance of eliminating unpleasant odors or enhancing exquisite smells as the only useful sensory motivators. This is not true.

In the expression, "Take time to smell the roses," we see evidence of the greater meaning of fragrance as part of the person's total environment—the motivational climate in which they work. Social scientists have experimented with environment as a motivator. However, little has been done to examine the use of the sense of smell as a motivator. There is growing evidence that this particular human sense has greater bearing on human motivation than we realize. If you are motivating a shopper to buy goods from your bakery, aroma can be critical to getting attention and urging them to buy. If you are motivating a person to work, this overall sense of environment affects work productivity.

Once again, attempt to find a way to use the sense of smell to send out value messages to others—to help motivate them. It is your role as the sensory motivator to devise methods which achieve this result.

SENSORY MOTIVATION IN TODAY'S WORLD

Today we are all dealing with a world that is ever-changing, composed of people with different values, cultures, ethics, needs and desires. People are more aware of the world around them than ever before in history. They are increasingly willing to challenge authority, to question. They are more mobile and transient, as transportation technology provides un-limited opportunities for personal and professional movement.

Family structures have changed. Interpersonal relationships have evolved into different and often conflicting value systems. So what is happening in the world today? Change. Human and technological change. Cultural change. Change in every aspect of our lives.

We need effective motivation to help us cope with the

turmoil of change. We need sensory motivation because utilizing the human senses is the most direct and effective way to break through to others. It helps others willingly to join us in a common quest for personal and professional success in the world of today and tomorrow.

The more human senses you utilize when trying to motivate others, the more successful you will be in helping them to help themselves.

PATRICK SWEENEY
P.O. Box 5784
Gold Coast Mail Center
4217 Queensland, Australia
075-502517

Patrick Sweeney

Patrick Sweeney of Australia is actively making a name for himself as a speaker and sales trainer.

He has worked in the area of Personal Development for over 8 years, running in excess of 700 self-improvement sessions and seminars on sales.

He has personally developed a large range of time-planning systems for management, self-employed and sales people. These programs are unique and, as Patrick puts it, "Give a tool that one can work with and help put into practise the great ideas that the orators and mentors promote."

He is rapidly building a network of distributors marketing his material and a range of selected products from speakers and companies from throughout the world.

These self-employed opportunities are an excellent platform for people who wish to make the step into sales training, seminar promotion and public speaking.

As a speaker he is known for his nuts and bolts presentations and gets his message through because of well-researched material and an enthusiastic presentation.

He has addressed groups in the U.S.A., Australia and New Zealand.

Four Dynamite D's of Motivation: DECIDE, DETERMINE, DO IT, DON'T QUIT

by Patrick Sweeney

*"Personally I'm always ready to learn,
although I do not always like being taught."*
—Winston Churchill

If you are like me, Churchill, you and I all have one thing in common. However, it follows that learning and personal motivation need to be synonymous if we are to enjoy enduring growth and personal satisfaction in our lives.

Often when we see or hear the word learning, it can spark a conscious or subconscious reaction with some of the less pleasant experiences of our school days. What I've found to be a more positive approach, is to replace the word learning with the short phrase "gaining experience." Establish our goals, then get out there and gain experience while progressing toward them. Every day we gain experience whether we like it or not.

Let's talk about a fresh approach to our goals. There's been a lot written, said and promoted on goal setting. Most of it is excellent but among some of the ideas I've tried hard to follow are a few foibles. They seem to trip me and others in spite of our diligent application.

Don't Tell!

The biggest and most classical misconception I've found promoted is the premise, "Tell the world your goals." If ever there was an ambush on the goal setter, that would have to be it. The well-meaning advocates of this idea either fall into a category mentioned shortly or just haven't done their homework.

The basis for the promotion of this unsuspecting, ankle-tripping idea, is the theory that by being outspoken about your goals, you are making a commitment you then have to live up to. Unfortunately, my many years of personal experience and observation in working closely with a wide spectrum of people in various types of motivationally oriented programs, have proven the contrary to be true. There is massive evidence to support this.

Many years ago I had a friend who was the greatest goal teller I've ever met. He would tell anyone who would listen his long, medium and short-term goals. How much he'd made, was making and intended to make. When things went wrong, he'd feel guilty. He was then obliged to go around and tell everyone what had happened. He spent more time keeping people up with his play, than in the game himself. He was team, referee and commentator all in one.

What I now know he was doing was satisfying his ego by expressing his concept of his potential. What he didn't realize was that he was depleting his ego of its drive. He tripped himself just as surely as if you take the fuel away from an engine. It can't perform. His ego was craving to be fed. He did it the easy way, with words, not with action. Today he is no better off than he was fifteen frustrating years ago.

After many years of following a similar but not quite so extravagant routine, I realized that I was filling my ego with air and not action. The people I admired and respected most, because of their likeable personalities and worthwhile achievements, kept their ambitions very close to their chests.

Show Them

Their ambitions were among their most precious possessions. They treated them accordingly. They didn't tell the world what they were going to do. They simply showed the world what they had done. That was how they satisfied their egos.

There are a few people who in their own right do the opposite. While starting from humble beginnings, they shout their goals from their rooftops every day and do achieve them. These unique and rare individuals are dynamic enough in their already well-developed make-up, to barge their way to the top. But with their arrogance of personality development and failure to consider the more sensitive needs of others, they often alienate themselves from many friends and worthwhile relationships along the way. It's been my observation that these exceptions to the rule are not the models which people like us of average ability can use as our mentors as we blaze our trail to the top.

Gain Experience

Many times it's been said that successful people are ordinary people who do ordinary things extraordinarily well. My way of relating to that is: "Successful people are ordinary people who took an ordinary idea or skill and stuck to it, gaining experience until they accomplish that one thing extraordinarily well."

John Walker, the world record-holder for a number of years for running the mile, told me that he learned early to keep his goals to himself. John worked in a quarry just outside Auckland, New Zealand. He set as one of his goals, winning the gold medal in the 1500 meters at the Montreal Olympics, five years before he hoped to achieve it. Every morning before work he would run several miles, again at lunch time, and once more at the conclusion of the day. When asked why by his work-mates, he'd tell them of his intention. He was ridiculed and laughed at. He quickly learned to keep his own council. He reserved his dreams only to those who could help him achieve his objectives.

In the five-year lead-up time, he kept his goal stored both in his conscious and subconscious mind. John covered over 25,000 miles of rigorous training—4.4 million steps to success! When his workmates chided or asked him why he was dedicating himself to this running, he would simply say, "One of these days I'll show you fellows something." One of those days he not only showed those fellows something but he revealed his goal to the world. He won the gold, and later on, broke both the indoor and outdoor mile record.

What Will You Do Extraordinarily Well?

Whatever you have decided it may be, then that should be your secret goal. Many people have as their goal the car, the house, the ranch, the million dollars or whatever. While these may be the things you want, when we apply what I call the greatest law in the universe—the law of cause and effect—many people find that their goal is an effect. This effect should actually be your motive for action. Your motivation to do your ordinary thing extraordinarily well.

Putting the ideas we're covering here into a formula may make it easier to work with. Here it is:

1. **Decide.** What ordinary thing you want to do extraordinarily well.
2. **Determine.** What the most exciting benefits of your expressed, but yet to be developed talent will bring you.
3. **Do it diligently.** Never stop "gaining experience" in making your talent show through.
4. **Don't quit.** As the immortal Winston Churchill put it so succinctly, "Never. Never. Never quit."

I like to add to the great Sir Winston's famous speech, some special words of my own. "Never. Never. Never quit thinking about your goals most of the time."

Over a number of years of trial and error, I have experimented with various approaches. I've found within myself and observed this trait in others that the thing which separated the achievers from the status quo is their *willingness to take risks.*

Risk is another word for price. Everything has a price. The greater the reward, the greater the price in terms of risk. If you try to undercut the price, you'll invariably finish up with an inferior reward. Remember, the Master has set the price of our accomplishment.

Three Types of Risks

Risk can generally be categorized under three simple headings. Stupid, practical and minor. When something has only minor risks, your personal satisfaction will be minor. Stupid risks usually end in heartbreak. Practical risks produce practical results.

It appears to me there is a set of scales in achievement. It always balances as far as potential rewards are concerned. Based on the risks you are currently taking, what are your potential rewards? This should not be confused, as some people tend to, with potentiality of the endeavor in its own right. An accurate assessment can only be derived from your appraisal of your risk involvement, weighed against practical results.

In dealing with risk, the biggest factor we must contend with is our childhood upbringing. Most of us, in the wisdom of our parents, were taught both directly and indirectly to avoid risk. But the reality of life is that to avoid risk is to avoid success.

Reality Thinking

Success has many meanings depending on the context in which it is used. The one that excites me the most is when success is associated with overcoming risks and bringing the idea to fruition. Risk also has its other side. It can also mean potential failure and, of course, if there is no potential failure, there can be no potential success. In this sphere, success and failure exist within risk.

Much has been written on being positive and optimistic. I can assure you in past years there has probably been no greater advocate of these ideas than me. But as steel is forged in the hottest fires and diamonds compressed from coal, I have had to modify my approach to what I now term reality thinking. Defeat is a reality, loss is a reality, not necessarily an end result, but a reality where it exists or potentially exists. Defeat has forced me to be much more pragmatic in my approach to life.

John Dewey, Charles Peirce and William James, the philosophers who gave form to the doctrines of pragmatism, claimed an idea could be said to "work" only when actions based upon it resulted in the predicted results.

We can spend a lifetime trying to get ideas to work and eventually fit a predictable process as described in the works of Dewey, James and Peirce. And so we should; not to make our life patterns absolute, but to be involved on a continuing basis in improving that which we have accomplished, while still taking on new challenges.

- Confront risk and you are confronting both the ingredients of success and failure.
- Conquer risk and you have conquered success in that which you are pursuing.

It is my opinion that there are many talented people in the world who are unsuccessful because of their reluctance to take risks. There are many potential champions who will never begin. Not because they don't dream, but because they stop dreaming when the dream enters the arena of risk.

Many times I'm asked to address groups of salespeople "who need motivating." In reality it is often the management, the example setters, who need the motivation. When sales aren't up to scratch, they think it's the salespeoples' fault. "Motivate them!"

In some instances that may be the case, but more often than not it's the inflexible management team, safe and secure in their corporate cocoons, who need motivating. They need to break out of their security syndrome and into the arena of risk, where the best that exists within us all has an opportunity to reveal itself. Risk drives us on to higher levels of personal satisfaction than we've ever experienced before.

Are you someone who has higher aspirations? Do you harbor an enduring desire to succeed, but cannot seem to get it together?

Come back to basics:

- **Decide.** What ordinary thing do you want to do extraordinarily well?
- **Determine.** What are the most exciting benefits your expressed, but yet to be developed talent will

bring you?

- **Do it and don't quit.** Never. Never. Never quit along the way.
- **Never. Never. Never** quit thinking about your goals most of the time.
- **Confront risk** with a practical but optimistic approach.

Choose to be Extraordinary

It's a simple formula and it works, learn it by heart, build a plan around it. Get stuck in and do it and you'll look back to see the day when you chose your ordinary thing that you will then do extraordinarily well. You'll have gained the necessary experience. You'll receive the benefits of being an outstanding individual who took complete responsibility for your cherished achievement and station in life.

Tools for Success

The short but practical and effective formula we've just covered, can and will give you virtually anything you choose for it to produce. But here is one added ingredient. This will guarantee your success and ensure that you will achieve your desires in the shortest possible time. But before I tell you about it, I'd like to share with you some tools for success. I've been involved with the development of these.

For a long time I've had the belief that there is plenty of information available through books, cassettes, courses, seminars, rallies, videos, films and magazines;

but too few tools to help put all this great bank of information and ideas into action.

As part of my plan that I want to do extraordinarily well, I have been developing such tools. With the widespread acceptance of these outstanding learning tools that's been achieved, the ongoing nature of my objective is being accomplished.

Unique Business Services (U.B.S.) now markets a range of success tools. These are planners, organizational aids, project plotters, prospecting systems, recruiting systems, marketing plans and a host of other great ideas. They are designed for use by entrepreneurs, business people, salespeople, management, executive and generally ambitious people. We also have some new aids for multilevel and party plan sales. You'll want to know more, so write to me personally at U.B.S., P.O. Box 5784, Gold Coast Mail Center, 4217 Queensland, Australia. (Also ask for a free introductory newsletter and a copy of the formula contained in this presentation; for your office or home.)

Now For That Something More

Most people plan their week with a To-Do list. They map out all the things that will lead to a successful week. All the people they need to contact, meetings to attend, functions, letters and activities. If you don't follow such a procedure, I highly recommend you consider starting.

Once you have made the list, go over it and examine it. See what else you can do with each activity to give more of yourself. It is right here that you can hit the bull's-eye by being able to exercise the great principle of "going the extra mile." It is a principle that is an integral but often overlooked part of the greatest law of the universe—Cause and Effect.

This part of the law has been stated in many ways; here are just a few ways it has been paraphrased:

- Do unto others as you would have them do unto you.
- Go the extra mile.
- The law of compensation.
- Give and you shall be given.
- Help thy brother's boat to shore.
- The law of increasing return.
- Be a go-giver if you want to become a go-getter.
- The degree that I help other people get what they want will be the degree that I will get what I want.
- My rewards in life will always be in direct proportion to the service I render and the people I help.

If you can give more of yourself than necessary in everything you do, you'll be weighing the scales of compensation so heavily in your favor you will be amazed. You will attract great things to you, although this may take some time to be revealed to you.

Should you not be satisfied that you are getting enough from life, start putting more in! Some people are putting such meagre effort into what they do, the scales balance very, very little by way of reward. They increasingly slide further and further behind both mentally and financially. Do your "something more." You'll be both surprised and delighted with the progress you can accomplish in a very short time.

Today is the day we are reaping yesterday's crop. If you want more of that crop today, it's too late; but it's not too late for tomorrow's crop. Today everything you say, think and do sow the very seeds that will grow into the failure or the marvel of tomorrow. Remember, too, it's always your future—always *your* move. Play the game right and you'll have a great forever.

"Men can alter their lives by altering their attitudes."

—William James

DEBRA HALPERIN OLSON
Yes to Success
P.O. Box 3728
Santa Monica, CA 90403
(213) 392-9608

Debra Halperin Olson

*Debra Halperin Olson is founder and
president of the national success seminar company,*
YES TO SUCCESS. *In the three years since she
founded her company, she has given hundreds of
lectures and seminars from coast to coast and has
appeared on radio and TV talk shows in every major
city in the United States. Some of those shows include*
Mid-Morning L.A.; Chicago Today; Good Morning,
New England; *and the noontime news in Des Moines,
Iowa! Her seminars attract businesspeople,
homemakers, educators, students, professionals—
people from all walks of life—and are now being
offered for some of the most prestigious companies in
the country. Prior to founding* YES TO SUCCESS,
*Debra enjoyed success as an investment advisor,
public relations executive and as a business
consultant.*

*Debra's sparkling personality and dynamic
enthusiasm, coupled with her thorough understanding
of the principles of achieving success, her outstanding
ability to communicate those principles and her
sincere belief that everyone can enjoy a successful and
happy life, make her one of the most sought-after
young professionals in the speaking industry today.*

*Married for six years to actor Mark Olson, Debra
finds time in her busy schedule to work out five times
a week, meditate twice a day and "read lots of
success books!" She has just completed her first tape
cassette album entitled, "It's Time to Say YES TO
SUCCESS."*

THE MOTIVATIONAL MAGIC OF SAYING YES TO SUCCESS

by Debra Halperin Olson

> *"If I am not for myself, then who will be for me?*
> *But if I am for myself alone, then what am I?*
> *And if not now, when?"*
>
> **—Hillel**

We are so lucky to be alive today. There's so much to learn. There's so much to do. So much to experience. To enjoy. To cherish. To become. Then why is it that only about five percent of the people in this great country of ours choose to grab hold of life and live it? Why is it that only a handful of people are willing to say, "Come on life. I'm ready. And I'm willing to do whatever needs to be done so that I can become the best person I can be and so that I can discover and fulfill my purpose for being here, and live a life I'm proud of."

I don't believe that people are lazy or disinterested or deliberately negative or consciously cynical. I believe that every human being is capable of great things. And I believe that people choose to remain in the 95 Percent Club (that 95 percent of the population who chooses to accept mediocrity as the status quo) only because they don't have the knowledge they need to join the 5 Percent Club. No one yet has shared with them the requirements for admission.

In this chapter I will share with you some of the things I've learned, some of the knowledge I've acquired about joining and remaining a member of the 5 Percent Club. But, of course, it's up to *you* what you do with this knowledge. The knowledge alone won't do it for you. *You* have to do it for yourself. Because contrary to what you may have heard in the past, knowledge is not power. Knowledge is only *potential* power; it's not power until you *use* it.

What Do You Really Want?

"Go for what you really want, not what you know you can get."
—Maharishi Mahesh Yogi

The first requirement for having what you want in life is to decide what it *is* you want. Simple. After all, you can't expect to get somewhere if you don't know where you're going. But too many of us spend so much time complaining about what we don't have or what we should have done, we have no energy left to think about what we want to have and what we are going to do.

Stop lamenting the past. It's over and done. Sure we made "mistakes" and we missed opportunities, but in reality there's no such thing as a mistake. Mistakes are only opportunities to learn what *not* to do next time. Mistakes don't happen just to make us suffer. Mistakes can be our greatest assets—*if* we don't react to them by feeling sorry for ourselves and giving up, but rather by seeing the lessons and growing better and stronger from them. If you *don't* learn the lessons, then the same mistakes, the same adversities will surface again and again. In Napolean Hill's book *Grow Rich with Peace of Mind,* he speaks of adversity as a stepping stone to greater opportunity. He says that when he sees adversity coming, he says to it, "Hello little fellow. I don't know what lesson it is you've come to teach me but, whatever it is, I will learn it so well that you will not have to come back a second time."

So, keeping in mind the cumulative knowledge of our past experiences, let's start fresh today and decide where we want to go from here.

What is it in your heart of hearts that you really want to be, to do, to have in this life? If you were totally honest and allowed yourself to think in terms of all possibilities and not in narrow, safe channels, what would you let yourself desire? As a matter of fact, I want you to put this book down for a few minutes and take out a piece of paper and write a long list of everything you truly desire.

For now, don't worry about *how* you're going to achieve these things, just let yourself think big and write what you really want, and not what you think you can easily get. In other words, if you really want to be the president of your company, don't write down, "Become floor manager." If you really want a Cadillac Seville, don't write down, "Have a new Ford Pinto Wagon." And if you really want to find your perfect mate and have a completely loving and full relationship, don't write, "Find a mate at least better than the last one." Let's work on these lists for about 10 minutes.

Okay, now you have your list—or at least five out of every hundred who read this chapter do. The rest of you said you'd do it later. And a few of you might—but most of you will never take this all-important first step unless you *do it now*. This 10-minute exercise can be one of the most important investments you'll ever make in your future success.

So now that a few more of you have your lists—and I hope you thought BIG!—I have a surprise for you. *You can have everything you wrote down.* That's right. You see, *inherent in the ability to have a desire is the ability to fulfill that desire.* Isn't that amazing? You are not capable of having a desire that you are not capable of fulfilling. Nature works in perfect ways. Nature doesn't trick us and say, "Well, I gave you that desire but, ha ha ha, I didn't give you the ability to fulfill it!" As Emerson says, "There's nothing capricious in Nature."

If you have a dream, if you have a goal deep in your heart, begin to realize it. Make the commitment, knowing that your goals want you as much as you want them. They're there waiting for you, even if they seem very far away and you can't see them yet. If you're in Los Angeles and you're on your way to Fairfield, Iowa—just because you're not in Fairfield yet, it doesn't mean that Fairfield doesn't exist! Your dreams are waiting for you—now—so let's not waste any more life. Let's start moving towards them today.

My Story

*"An aim in life is the only fortune worth finding;
and it is not to be found in foreign lands, but in
the heart itself."*
—**Robert Louis Stevenson**

Let me tell you a little about myself. I don't have any
rags to riches story to share. I didn't grow up in poverty.
On the contrary, I've always had pretty much everything
I wanted, and certainly everything I needed. I didn't have
a family that told me I wouldn't amount to anything. In
fact, my parents were (and are) the two most loving,
generous, kind and supportive people on earth; my
brother's love and admiration for me is surpassed only by
my love and admiration for him; and my husband, well, I
give thanks every day for whatever I did to deserve a man
like Mark. I've never really experienced what I'd call a
"low" point in life—any time of great desperation or
depression or unhappiness. Again, quite to the contrary,
when I was a teenager I began to practice the Tran-
scendental Meditation (TM) program which is a simple,
scientific, nonreligious technique that provides deep rest
to the body which releases stress and fatigue, but at the
same time enlivens the mind. The results of practicing
the TM technique for me have been not only perfect
health and clear thinking, but also deep and lasting inner
silence and stability.

So my life has been good—but, you see, an easy life is
not always the most powerful motivator. History has
shown us that most great people have come from
backgrounds of considerable adversity. Think of some

truly great people and who comes to mind? Abraham Lincoln. Franklin Roosevelt. Helen Keller. Ludwig von Beethoven. Their adversity developed in them a burning desire, a commitment to succeed like Scarlet O'Hara's commitment that "I will never be hungry again." Given my background, it could have been very easy for me to follow the beaten path and lead my life without taking any real risks. But inside I knew that in order to have a really successful life, you have to be true to yourself, even if it means "marching to the beat of a different drummer, however measured or far away" (Henry David Thoreau). And there comes a point in all of our lives when we have to ask ourselves, "Am I really fulfilling my purpose for being here? Am I really happy? Am I really listening to my inner drummer?"

These questions begin to present themselves to me several years ago when I was comfortably employed as an account executive for a financial company in Los Angeles. And when the questions came, I knew that the answers must not be far behind.

One of my co-workers at this financial company was a man very much involved in attending motivational seminars. Based on his recommendation, the company agreed to pay for any seminar which the employees desired to attend so long as it was perceived to be a potential tool to increase our productivity and effectiveness. Thus I had the opportunity to attend countless seminars: seminars on time management, on creating a successful image, on attitude, on sales techniques—on everything you could think of and a few things you couldn't.

Then one day I was visiting a friend who was attending a small university in the Midwest. She told me there was a man on campus who was giving a seminar on prosperity. I wasn't interested in attending at first; after all, what could he possibly teach me that I didn't know? I had been to so many seminars, and I had already read *Think and Grow Rich!* But because my friend was uncharacteristically insistent, my intuition told me I should go.

Chris (the seminar leader) turned out to be a warm and sincere man, not the high-powered "let's conquer the world" type. But even within the first few minutes I knew I was there for a reason. He told us that work should be nourishing, not draining. He said that if you feel drained at the end of the day, you are probably doing the wrong work. He made the analogy that having a career that's not really right for you is like buying a coat that doesn't quite fit—no matter what you do, you will never feel really comfortable in it. And then he said that until you find the work you really love, you won't feel totally successful—even if you gain all the fame and fortune in the world. I knew he had hit the nail on the head.

Now that I had this knowledge, I knew that I had to make a commitment to myself to seek out and find that work which would provide the key to my real success and happiness. It had never dawned on me before that we all deserve to have more in life than a reasonably likeable job and an income to match.

When I returned to Los Angeles, I told my husband Mark what I had learned at the seminar and the commitment I had made to myself. Infected by my enthusiasm, he suggested that we immediately sit down at the kitchen table and start to write out our lifetime goals. Soon Mark was scribbling away purposefully, with a little smile on his face. Mark is one of those fortunate people who has a great talent and great sense of purpose. He is an accomplished, versatile actor, and this talent has been his guiding force for many years. He has his goals clearly in view: progressing though the steps of commercial acting, onward to the stage and screen, and ultimately—an Oscar, an Emmy, *and* a Tony. He just *knows* exactly what he wants. But I, on the other hand, sat looking at him writing away with such enthusiasm and clarity that I almost began to cry. "Why isn't it easy for me to find *my* . . . something . . . that I want to do? Why don't *I* have a passion for anything?" I knew one thing for sure: I had no passion for being an account executive for a financial company. It just wasn't satisfying to my inner self; it just wasn't *me*. But what was this elusive "something," my own special purpose in life? I was stumped.

"Sweetheart, just do that exercise that you learned from Chris," Mark suggested. "Just start writing down everything you enjoy doing. If you could have your ideal career, what elements would it have?" I reflected for a moment and then began to list the things I liked to do. The list looked like this:

Number One: Talk.
Number Two: Do something *good* for people, and be involved in a product I could believe in and guarantee.

Number Three: Be self-employed so I could go to the beach whenever I wanted and take off for the health club without asking anybody's permission.

Number Four: Be financially successful.

Number Five: Have a job that involves public speaking and appearing on radio and TV talk shows.

Number Six: Do something with all the success principles I had been learning in the seminars I was attending.

Although I didn't yet see my ideal career embodied in these six points, writing down all the components was a powerful experience. Doing the exercise gave me a strong feeling of moving closer to the clear knowledge of my purpose in life. An almost physical "clicking" was going on in my brain, like that "aha" experience when the elements of a math problem start fitting together and the solution is almost there.

When I finished writing, I just let go and went to bed. The *very next morning* I was sitting down in a quiet moment, and the idea came to me: Establish a company . . . Offer seminars on how to become successful in all areas of life . . . Combine all the knowledge and experience you've gained in your professional life with the extensive information you acquired at all of the many seminars you attended. Create a seminar of your own that would provide a step-by-step program on how to decide on worthy goals, make the plans to reach them, manage your time effectively, create a successful image, understand money, and develop an attitude that supports fulfillment of all your desires. Yes, have your own business! Go on radio and TV. Become financially successful; and talk all you want!

As soon as I had the idea, I started working on it. When you have an idea that fills a need or answers a lack in society—go for it. Don't wait until you think you're ready, because if you wait until you think you're ready, you'll never really think you're ready. Ideas come to us because the time is right for them to be fulfilled. These ideas want to manifest themselves through you. But if you don't act on these ideas, then they will go to somebody else who will. Have you ever had a great idea and not done anything about it and then a year later you hear about someone becoming a millionaire or a Nobel Prize winner for that same idea? Ideas are the starting point of all great achievement—and the road to failure is paved with great ideas that are never acted on.

Making the Commitment

"For a web begun, God sends the thread."
—Anonymous

Starting is the only hard part. After we get over what's called in physics the "point of inertia" the rest is really quite simple—almost automatic—since a body in motion tends to stay in motion. Once we make the commitment to our own success, it seems that all of creation rallies around that commitment.

Think about what happened in your own life the last time you made a definite commitment to something— let's say, some project. As soon as you said, "Okay, I'll do it," didn't everything begin to fall into place? People showed up. Money appeared. All kinds of circumstances occurred to support the decision.

The great German philosopher Goethe had this to say about commitment:

> "Until one is committed, there is hesitating, the chance to draw back, always ineffectiveness. Concerning all acts of initiative and creation there is one elementary truth: That the moment one definitely commits oneself, the entire Providence moves. All sorts of things begin to occur to help one that would never otherwise have occurred. A whole stream of events issues forth from the decision, raising in one's favor all manner of unforeseen incidents and events and material assistance that no man would have dreamed would come his way."

Taking a Risk

> "If you don't risk anything, you risk even more."
>
> **—Erica Jong**

I realize that making a commitment to achieving some new goal involves taking a risk, but greatness always involves moving beyond our comfort zone. If you take a risk, yes, there's a chance you might fail. But if you *don't* take a risk, there's *no* chance you'll succeed.

The problem with us adults is that we're so afraid of failure—mainly of looking bad in front of our peers—that we avoid any situations where the degree of risk is high. We're so afraid of making a mistake that we end up making the biggest mistake of all—*the mistake of not trying.*

Sure, you can remain a member of the 95 Percent Club—being content with the status quo and not running the risk of failure—but is that a life you can really be proud of? It is better to attempt to do great things and fail, than to attempt to do nothing and succeed.

In the words of Theodore Roosevelt:

> *"It is not the critic who counts; not the man who points out how the strong man stumbled, or where the doer of deeds could have done them better. The credit belongs to the man who is actually in the arena, whose face is marred by dust and sweat and blood; who strives valiantly, who errs and comes short again and again; who knows the great enthusiasms, the great devotions; who spends himself in a worthy cause; who at the best, knows in the end the triumph of high achievement, and who, at the worst, if he fails, at least fails while daring greatly, so that his place shall never be with those timid souls who know neither victory or defeat."*

You just have to keep in mind that there is really no such thing as failure. There are just different ways to learn how *not* to do a thing.

When Thomas Edison was busily inventing the incandescent light bulb, he logged over 1,000 unsuccessful attempts. When someone asked him how it felt to have failed 1,000 times, his reply was, "I never failed; I just discovered 1,000 ways how the light bulb would not work. And *every* attempt brought me closer to the knowledge of how it would." He succeeded on his 1,001st try.

Use *action* to defeat worry and fear. Once you *do* that thing you were afraid of, you'll see it was all a mirage. In your mind, it was scary. In reality, it was simple. As Ralph Waldo Emerson said, "Do the thing you fear and the death of fear is certain."

Keeping Your Dreams Safe

> *"Man who says it can't be done should not interfere with man who is doing it."*
> **Chinese Proverb**

Here is another important principle of success: Be careful with whom you share your cherished goals. It's a good idea to keep them to yourself until you are well on your way to accomplishing them.

When I started my company, I kept my idea secret for quite a while. I didn't share it with anyone except my husband because I knew that he would be completely supportive. While your goals are still delicate seeds that can easily be crushed, keep them protected by keeping them to yourself. Otherwise, even the most well-meaning friends and relatives might say something like: "Oh, honey, you'll never be able to do that . . . it's a tough world out there . . . there's so much competition . . . why don't you just appreciate the job you have now . . ." After the seeds are planted, watered and growing strong, then you can go ahead and tell the whole world.

And if it should happen that someone tries to dissuade you from your goal, well, just don't let anyone tell you what you won't be able to do. Turn every criticism into an inspiration to work even harder. You're the only one who knows what you're capable of achieving. Listen to your own heart. No one else's opinion really matters.

When Henry Ford had the idea to build the Model T, he went to his father and told him the plan. His father replied, "And you gave up a good $25 a week job to chase a crazy idea like that?" Think where we'd be today if Henry had said, "You know, Dad, you're right . . ."

Say Yes to Success

"If you let go of your dreams, you die."
Flashdance

Finally, you must believe that the good you want is on its way. Assume it's coming. There is no reason to doubt. If you're going to doubt anything, doubt the doubts.

In the movie, *The Empire Strikes Back,* there's a scene where Luke Skywalker gets his spaceship stuck in the mud. He tries to get it out, and after many attempts goes in and tells Yoda that he's doomed; he'll *never* get home now.Yoda keeps assuring him it will be no problem, they'll get the spaceship out and he'll be on his way. To which Luke replies, "No, Yoda, you don't understand. I'm *never* going to get home." At that point Yoda looks at Luke, waddles out of his hut and over to the pond where, without moving a muscle, just using his mind, he lifts up the spaceship and moves it over onto the dry land. Luke stares at the phenomenon and then says to Yoda, "I saw you do that, Yoda, and I *still* don't believe it." And Yoda replies, "That is why you have failed."

You must believe that if you have a dream, it's just a matter of time before it becomes a reality. Just never lose sight of your dreams and never settle for less than what you really want. Be persistent, but also be patient. Move quickly, but never be in a hurry. And always remember to take at least one step closer to your goals every day and promise yourself—right now—that you will never give up.

> *"If one advances confidently in the direction of his dreams, and endeavors to live the life which he has imagined, he will meet with a success unexpected in common hours. If you have built castles in the air, your work need not be lost. That is where they should be. Now put the foundations under them."*
>
> **—Henry David Thoreau**

May you enjoy all great success. You deserve it!

"Live neither in the past nor in the future, but let each day's work absorb all your interest, energy and enthusiasm. The best preparation for tomorrow is to do today's work superbly well . . ."

—Sir William Osler

POSITIVE PAUL STANYARD

Happyrich Enterprises
6013 Susan Court
San Jose, CA 95123
(408) 225-7424

"Positive Paul" Stanyard

Positive Paul is known as the "Doctor of Positivity," who has formulated this new and exciting way of living is called "Positivity."

"Positivity is rethinking and reversing negative things and ideas in a new way to creatively develop people, place and product." Positive Paul will come into your life or company and rethink and reverse anything negative with your people, your place of business and your product. He will do this on a one-to-one basis or with groups of people. He will do this any place in the world. Positive Paul guarantees that he can turn anything negative into positive creativity. His Doctorate has come from 30 years of teaching human relations, applied psychology, advertising, salesmanship and public speaking. Positive Paul is co-author of three books, The Great Persuaders, The Magnificent Motivators *and* Build a Better You. *He gives talks on "The Psychology of Mike Todd," "The Happyrich," "Selling," "Self-Confidence," "Creative Living," "Advertising," "Depression," "Memory Techniques," "Acro-action," and "Goalsearching."*

He has made cassette tapes called "Happyrich Secrets to Success and Wealth," "Yes I Can," "Acronyms . . . The Key to Motivation," "Let's Put Sell and Sales Back into Selling," "How to Know What You Really Want, How to Get What You Really Want."

ACRONYMS:
The Key to Motivation and Memory
by *Positive Paul Stanyard*

"Smooth words make smooth ways."

—**W.G. Benham**

Acronyms have served as handy communication and memory shortcuts for centuries. They date back to ancient Rome. An acronym is a word formed from the first letters of other words. It was in our fast-paced atmosphere of the twentieth-century that acronyms got their big boost. The years of the New Deal produced many acronyms. NRA for **N**ational **R**ecovery **A**dministration. WPA for **W**orks **P**rogress **A**dministration, and so forth. World War II brought new weapons, new codes and a population explosion of acronyms. In fact before World War II the word acronym didn't exist. It was during this period that the word was coined and first used in February, 1943. New acronyms were formed to save precious inches of newsprint and precious seconds of broadcast time. Acronyms were brought on to serve as cloaks of military secrecy and as spotlights on products, ideas and programs which the public was expected to support.

An acronym is usually read or spoken as a single word, rather than letter by letter. RADAR for **R**adio **D**etection **A**nd **R**anging. There are some acronyms that are verbalized letter by letter, rather than used as a single word. PO for **P**ost **O**ffice. RPM for **R**evolutions **P**er **M**inute. There has been a fast growth of this new acronym language. In 1960 there were 12,000 acronyms listed in the Acronym Dictionary and today there are well over 200,000 listed and being used. And I find no slowdown in the pace at which this modern acronym language is growing.

Acronyms Will Improve Memory

Acronyms have been a motivational hobby of mine since 1952. That's the year I took the Dale Carnegie Course in Public Speaking and Human Relations. I was introduced to my first acronym at the first meeting. We were being conducted through a contest in remembering names. The instructor told us that there were three basic principles to all memory.

They are impression, repetition and association. He

went on to explain that we could remember the three memory techniques by remembering a man's name, IRA. The **I** stood for impression, the **R** stood for repetition and the **A** stood for association. IRA was my first acronym. That was in 1952, and I have been collecting and creating acronyms for over 30 years. In all that time I still remember my second and third acronyms that I originated. HASP is an acronym for the four subjects that I decided to study and master to become a professional author and speaker. Those four subjects are **H**uman Relations, **A**pplied Psychology, **S**alesmanship, and **P**ublic Speaking. The third acronym was an unknown word that I made up so that I could remember the definition of LUCK. The acronym is LIPMO, say it . . . "Lip'mo." It stands for **L**uck **I**s **P**reparation **M**eeting **O**pportunity.

So now whenever the subject of luck comes up in a conversation, I remember that luck is preparation meeting opportunity. I even made a meaningful motivational sentence of the word acronym itself. ACRONYM is for "**A**cronyms **C**an **R**einforce **O**ur **N**onproductive **Y**esterday **M**emory."

For many years I used acronyms to reinforce my poor memory. My first real test on using acronyms for motivation and memory came in 1955 when I was named Number One newspaper advertising salesperson in Pennsylvania, New Jersey, Delaware and Maryland. I was asked to fly to Harrisburg and give a 45-minute talk on How to Sell Advertising. By that time in my life I had decided to use acronyms to remember the outline and points of various talks I was giving in the Pittsburgh area.

By creating acronyms for my talks, I didn't have to carry notes or memorize anything. Acronyms don't guarantee that you'll give a good speech . . . they only guarantee that you'll remember what to say. Once you acronym the points of your talk, it gives you the confidence, the memory and the motivation to walk boldly to center stage and take command of the greatest show on earth.

The acronym that I used in Harrisburg that year was SELL. The S stood for See a lot of people. The E stood for Enthusiasm makes the difference. The first L stood for Learn that selling is 98% understanding human beings and 2% product knowledge. The second L stood for Lots of ideas, ideas and service. Under See a lot of people, I talked about fifteen different ways to see a lot of people. Under Enthusiasm makes the difference, I talked about ten exciting things they could do to become more enthusiastic than they are now. Under Learn that selling is 98% understanding human beings and 2% product knowledge, I reminded them of the many human relation principles that should be practiced to become a professional salesperson. Under Lots of ideas, ideas and service, I pointed out that the buyer of our products and services wanted ideas, ideas and good service.

Customers want ideas on how to satisfy their dominant buying motives. They want good news; ideas on how to increase their net profits. After the last L in SELL, I ended my talk with a summary . . . and then I was presented the trophy for the Number One salesperson of four states. The talk was a success. My confidence and self-esteem were very high. I heard several comments about, "It's no wonder that he's Number One" to "How can he remember all those facts and figures?"

From the one talk at Harrisburg that day, came an offer to take the position of Advertising Director of a group of newspapers in Delaware and Maryland. Just think, a new position came from one speech, and that speech came from one acronym . . . SELL! I have a special book in which I have recorded 315 motivational acronyms. I have spent 10,000 hours in 30 years putting these acronyms together. But hold on . . . the best is yet to come.

You are about to read a very inspiring, motivational and creative story of how I discovered a guaranteed action method to make people do the things they already know they should do. The method took years to slowly develop into the most unique system in the world for making people do the things that they dream and plan to do but never get done. It all came from the little word acronym and my dogged determination to make myself do the many things that I had planned for my life.

I personally like to develop new motivational words. I get so tired of using the same old phrases that have been used for three hundred years. You know how it is when you discover something new. When you create a new word or system that motivates you . . . it's a part of you. Excitement is high. Self-esteem is high. You can't wait for morning to come so you can get up and start the day with your new energy and creativeness. You fly through the air with happiness wings. Everyone you see is a wonderful person. The sun is beautiful. The trees are beautiful. It's exhilirating just to walk outside your own home, look

up to the sky, fling your arms wide open and shout . . .
"Look out little world, here I come."

We all have the power and freedom to choose to be
motivated or not to be motivated. We all have the power
and freedom to choose to get into action or just cope
with life as the normal people do. We have the power and
freedom to choose to set concrete, affirmative, realistic,
specific targets with target dates and have the happiness
and money we want.

The new guaranteed action method to get things
done is called *"Acro-action."* I creatively put the words
acronym and action together. It's a new word. It's never
been seen before. It's creative. It's unique. It's the key to
motivating yourself to get into action. Here's the
definition:

> *"Acro-action is the highest degree of self-
> motivation and action toward personal
> goals using acronyms as the key to self-
> starting action and a daily support
> system."*

Acro-action can keep you motivated simply by
inventing your own acronyms. Repeat them to yourself
many times during the day. These words act as
inspiration to get you started on some action every day
toward your 30-day goal. They are inner-motivational
reminders that keep you up, keep you goal directed, and
also act as a support system.

ACTION Is an Acronym for
Always Complete The Immediate Objective Now

When you think the word ACTION several times a day,

you will automatically think of the phrase, **A**lways **C**omplete **T**he **I**mmediate **O**bjective **N**ow. This acronym-phrase will be your inspiration and motivation to get into action *now*. Here's another short acronym . . . PEP. It means **P**ositive **E**nergetic **P**ersonality. PEP! **P**ositive **E**nergetic **P**ersonality. Can you feel what it does to you? It makes you feel peppy, positive and energetic . . . it's wonderful. PEP!!!

About a year ago I stopped using the word acronym. I created another key word called "Acro-gem." Why do I use "Acro-gem"? Simply because I enjoy creating new words and new ways to motivate myself. I want to create new ways to get and stay excited about life. "Acro-gem" is a new key word to motivation. Here's the definition: "An Acro-gem is a motivating word or short sentence formed from the first letters of other inspiring and meaningful words."

"Acro-Gems"

The word acronym is just a word. But . . . look at the word "Acro-gem" . . . it means a *motivating* word or short sentence. It's something personal. It's personal motivation. Look at it again . . . Acro-gem, it's a gem and it's an acronym. It's precious mind/brain stuff. Now I will tell you the new and complete definition of "Acro-action," the key to motivation and action. "Acro-action is the highest degree of self-motivation and action toward personal goals using Acro-gems as the key to self-starting action and daily support system." Let's be more creative and break down the word Acro-gems and make a phrase out of it. "**A**cro-gems **C**an **R**einforce **O**ur **G**oals, **E**nthusiasm, **M**otivation (and) **S**uccesses."

Acro-action is a new philosophy of action and support. There are many principles, laws and secrets of self-motivation. Napoleon Hill and his Mastermind group, W. Clement Stone and his PMA, Earl Nightingale and his Strangest Secret, The Treasure Map, Kopmeyer and his Goal Commands, pictures of role-models, self help books, records, tapes, self-hypnosis, support teams, affirmations, cybernetics, visualization and the greatest of them all . . . *ACTION!!!*

Now we have another key to motivation, another self-helper and a better way to personal action. By the way, KEY is the Acro-gem and I'm happy to say that I got this one from our publisher, Dottie Walters. (I love her.) KEY stands for **K**eep **E**ncouraging **Y**ourself! One way to keep encouraging yourself is repeat Acro-gems to yourself during the day. Another way to self-encouragement is to "five-sense" your past successes.

"Five-sensing" your past successes simply means to relax and see, hear, smell, taste and touch the many large and small successes that you have accomplished. The fun of this new philosophy called Acro-Action is that it can be personal. You can make up your own Acro-gems. You can be as creative as you want to be. Acro-gems are internal and external. You can keep them in your mind/brain, ready for instant inspiration. You can keep them pinned to the walls of your STP room. STP stands for **S**tudy-**T**hinking-**P**lanning room. You can get a blank book and start your private collection of Acro-gems. You can do anything your little motivational heart desires . . . but do something with the one life you have to live.

After birth, normal people have only 29,200 days to live on space ship Earth. That's because they live in "when" time. "When I get out of school I'll be happy." "When I get married." "When we have the first child, it will save our marriage." "When we have two cars." "When we take that vacation." You see, normal people never live today . . . they live in "when" time. Their life seems so short because they never really *live*. "When" never happens.

But look at the no-limit people. After birth they have 80 years to live on space ship Earth. Their life seems long because they live in "now" time. Today . . . this experience . . . this sunrise . . . this sunset. Be a no-limit person. There is no such word in your psychological vocabulary as "tomorrow." Think it, feel it, believe it. I can still remember the first secret of success that I read in an old torn brown book that was published over 60 years ago. "Simply do the things that you already know you should do, and don't do the things that you already know you shouldn't do." When do you do them? Today . . . today . . . today!!! Not tomorrow.

That brings us back to the subject of action through Acro-gems. Everyone needs a constant motivation-reminder because all motivation is self-motivation. It comes from inside. No one can do it for you. It's an attitude no person can really explain. When a person is truly motivated, it's almost as if he's outside his own body. He feels himself to be at the best of his powers, using all his capacities to the fullest. He feels .fully functioning, more intelligent, more perceptive, wittier, stronger, or more graceful than at other times. He or she is at their best. Acro-gems will keep you motivated when you use them every day.

Acro-Gem Your Way To Motivation

Here are some of my favorite Acro-gems. Memorize them and use them to keep yourself motivated. GOALS is an Acro-gem for **G**olden **O**pportunities **A**llowing **L**arge **S**uccess. If you say GOALS several times a day and think of the phrase that it stands for, this will help keep your mind on your goals.

ENTHUSIASM is an Acro-gem for **E**nthusiasm **N**eeds **T**he **H**igh **U**nseen **S**trength **I**nvolved **A**round **S**elf **M**otivation. It means that your enthusiasm comes from, and needs the power and strength of Self-Motivation. Find something that motivates you, sets you on fire, gets you jumping . . . then you'll find enthusiasm. THRIFT is an Acro-gem for the phrase, **T**ithing **H**abit **R**eflects **I**ndependence **F**or **T**omorrow. Every time money crosses your palms . . . think THRIFT. The Acro-gem phrase will come to mind and will motivate you to tithe 10% of your gross income. Tithe whom? Yourself . . .

that's whom you tithe. The Acro-gem will remind you to pay yourself first and live on the 90% that's left. At age 59 you'll have a million dollars. PRAYER is an Acro-gem for the phrase **P**eace **R**elaxation **A**nd **Y**our **E**ternal **R**adiance. When you think of the Acro-gem PRAYER you will be reminded that in prayer you find peace, relaxation and your eternal radiance. TNT is an Acro-gem for **T**oday **N**ot **T**omorrow. Every time you say TNT, that's your key to motivate you to get started on some powerful action.

Every time you make a mistake say "SOS." That's an Acro-gem for **S**eeds **O**f **S**uccess. Well . . . isn't that what a mistake is . . . a seed of success? IBM is **I**deas **B**ecome **M**oney. TAP, TAP, TAP is **T**ake **A**ction **P**ersistently, **T**ake **A**ction **P**ersistently, **T**ake **A**ction **P**ersistently. The next time you start to greet somebody with a "Good Morning," stop . . . don't do it; instead say, "Hi Fred, I've got ESP." And then tell him that ESP stands for **E**nergy, **S**trength, **P**ower. COPE is a good one. **C**hange **O**ur **P**ersonal **E**ffectiveness. MODEST . . . **M**en **O**f **D**ecency **E**arn **S**uccess **T**oday. Be an ACE, **A**ction **C**reates **E**nthusiasm. Did you ever look at a sunset and say, "WOW"? That WOW stands for **W**orld **O**f **W**onders. RAW! RAW! RAW! is an Acro-gem for **R**isk **A**nd **W**in, **R**isk **A**nd **W**in, **R**isk **A**nd **W**in!

Are you getting excited about Acro-gems? Can you feel the newness, the enthusiasm, the motivation? That's good, because the power and opportunities are open to you. It's a new and creative system that will keep you self-motivated every day. You can get the thrilling habit of originating your own keys to motivation. As you do your own Acro-gems, they will motivate you even more because they are yours. They come from inside you. They come from your heart's touchstone and they mean something to you. Motivation . . . it's wonderful. It has to be what makes the world go 'round.

Use Acro-Gems As Your Notes When Giving A Talk

When you use Acro-gems to remember the points of a talk, you are motivated by confidence. You have less fear with Acro-gems. Notes can be lost . . . but you never loose the notes in your mind if you form an Acro-gem from the points you want to cover. My real confidence in public speaking came when I started using Acro-gems. I knew I would never forget what to say . . . and that gives you confidence. Here's an example of an Acro-gem that I use constantly when giving a talk about confidence and self-esteem. BE CONFIDENT is the Acro-gem. And this is the way you should see it in your mind as you're giving the talk.

B . . . Become an expert in one thing.
E . . . Enjoy past successes to build self-esteem now.

C . . . Courses. Take all public speaking courses.

O . . . Only one you since time began and for eternity.

N . . . No can be very positive, *if* used the right way.

F . . . Form habit of paying yourself first with 10%

I . . . Invest $1,000 a year on books, tapes, seminars.

D . . . Dare to be different than normals and neurotics.

E . . . Enthusiasm builds self-confidence.

N . . . Nerve to do it right, do it wrong, but do it.

T . . . Take charge of your own life.

There are 11 points to my talk. I talk 5 or 6 minutes on each one. I give a few examples from my own life. The talk lasts for one hour and the audience loves it. Can't you just feel my confidence as I end my talk and I hear that wonderful applause? How proud I am of myself. I had no notes. I spoke from the heart. An hour's talk from one Acro-gem . . . BE CONFIDENT. And I chalked up another successful experience that I can draw strength from during my "Affirmation-Relaxation Time" in my STP Room every morning. Isn't it wonderful . . . this thing called motivation?

You can build Acro-gems from almost anything. Even the alphabet.

ABC . . . **A**ction **B**uilds **C**onfidence

DEF . . . **D**ecisions **E**rase **F**ailure

GHI . . . **G**oals **H**elp **I**nspiration

JKL . . . **J**umpers **K**eep **L**osing

MNO . . . **M**oney **N**eeds **O**bjectivity

PQR . . . **P**ersistence **Q**uietly **R**ewards

STU . . . **S**ucceed **T**hrough **U**sefulness

VWX . . . **V**ision **W**ithout **X**rays

YZ . . . **Y**our **Z**ero-hour (time to get started)

Isn't it fun? You can do it . . . just try. I will give you as many Acro-gems as space allows. Please use them for inspiration and motivation in your life. Use them for speaking in front of groups of people. Use them as selling points in a sales presentation. Use them for all types of memory.

ID . . . Individual Desire

DNA . . . Distorted Negative Attitude

DOPE . . . Dreams Of People Erased

AIDES . . . Acting Image Does Effect Success

MAP . . . Mission And Purpose

POP . . . Power Of Purpose

I AM . . . Ideas Are Money

HOT . . . Habits Of Thought

BAM . . . Be Action Minded

FATE . . . Fortune Alters The Event

ATTITUDE . . . Affirm Thoughts That Implant The Ultimate Desired Emotion

POISED . . . Posture Of Individual Success Every Day

GUILT . . . Giving Up Illusions Leaves Truth

BLAHS . . . Becoming Lackadaisical Accelerates Human Suffering

LUCK . . . Learned, Understood, Cultivated Knowledge

POSITIVE . . . People Of Success Initiate Thrilling Individual Victories Everyday

NEGATIVE . . . Negative Elements Give All Things Impossible Victory Early

FAST . . . First Action Step Today

ASS . . . Approval Seeking Sensitivity

GUTS . . . Getting Unlimited Tasks Started

PIC . . . **P**riority **I**s **C**hoice
IF . . . **I**magined **F**uture
CAN . . . **C**onstant **A**chievement **N**ow
ASK . . . **A**lways **S**eek **K**nowledge
BE . . . **B**oldly **E**xpect
DO . . . **D**iscipline **O**urselves
POPULAR . . . **P**eople **O**f **P**ower **U**se **L**ove **A**ppreciation
            Recognition
MAGIC . . . **M**ake **A** **G**reat **I**nternal **C**ommitment

There are acronyms, and there are Acro-gems . . . but remember that an acronym is just any old word, while an *Acro-gem* is a key to motivation. It's a motivating word or short sentence formed from the first letters of other inspiring and meaningful words. They have to mean something to you personally.

I am known as Positive Paul, "Doctor of Positivity." I have studied and researched success and motivation 2 hours a day, 7 days a week for 30 years. I have the equivalent of five college degrees or 22,000 hours studying success and motivation. There is one thing that I know to be true. "The more that I know, the more I know that I don't know." It's a daily quest to read, study, know, read, study, know. It will go on to the day that I graduate from this huge spaceship called Earth to a new dimension. In the meantime, you and I have to give it all we can.

Life is too long to be doing something we aren't happy about. A lot of people will disagree with me . . . but happiness is a goal. It's the most important goal or target we should aim for. Happiness is the most important thing in life. In fact, it's the only thing. The key is to find out the things that make you happy and do them right or do them wrong. But *do* them. Happiness is achievement. Achievement is action. Action is motivation and motivation is attitude. Or it is the other way around? Happiness is attitude. Attitude is motivation. Motivation is action and action is achievement . . . and we're right back to achievement is happiness! If you don't believe happiness is achievement . . . what about the man or woman who is sitting around doing nothing . . . are they truly happy? Try it sometime; sit around the house for a week . . . you'll be unhappy and depressed.

I'm sure I will be talking to you soon, but in the meantime I'll give you the definition of positivity. I don't think it will change the world . . . but it is a new philosophy that has changed my world. That's all that matters. Maybe it will help change your world and add some motivation to the many things that you want to do.

"Positivity is rethinking and reversing the negative in a new way to creatively develop people, place and product." As the Doctor of Positivity I am devoting my life to rethinking and reversing all negatives to develop the whole person, place and product. Positive motivation through Acro-gems is just one of the many creative ideas I have developed through the new success philosophy called Positivity. The word Positivity came from the two words positive and creativity. Positive . . . meaning the good, the true, the beautiful and the yesses of life, and the word creativity meaning the making of the new or rearranging the old in a new way.

Money is not motivation. A new car is not motivation.

A self-help book on motivation is not motivation. Motivation is not the "thing in itself" that you want. Motivation is the "why" you want what you want. Why do you want the money? Why do you want the new car? Why do you want the book? It's never "what" you want . . . it's always why do you want it? When you can answer that question, you have the key to your motivation. Remember the word KEY . . . it is an Acro-gem for **K**eep **E**ncouraging **Y**ourself.

Many people are not finding the motivation they want. The reason for this failure is everyone is acting like everyone else. We are a society of copycats. We conform to the way we think other people want us to act and be. Many of us are afraid to go out on our own . . . to act like ourselves. To be an individual and not pay attention to what "they" say. The one thing that will keep you motivated is being an individual. *Be yourself.* God made an original when he made you.

You will do things in your lifetime that no other person has ever done, and no other person will ever do. Your great motivation will come when you don't adjust to other people and their opinions. Always remember, you have the power, the ability and the right to look any person in the face and say, "No, thank you." Being motivated means becoming what you want to be and what you need to be. The sooner you show your originality the sooner your motivation will come. If you have an urge to do something else, that's your individuality trying to come to the surface. Follow that urge. The world needs your service, your originality and your motivation. All great companies started in the creative mind of one person with courage to do their own thing in their own way.

Get the habit of not letting outward events and other people tell you how to feel and act. The success type person who shows individuality is a person who isn't like everyone else. They're not afraid of change. They're not afraid of anything new and unusual. They're not afraid to do things alone. The important thing is doing what *you* want to do.

Acro-gems can be your key to motivation. Acro-gems used the right way will give you the motivation to do it right, do it wrong . . . but *do* it. Live . . . live . . . live . . . for God's sake LIVE. I love you. Please call or write!

"Things may come to those who wait, but only the things left by those who hustle."

—Abraham Lincoln

ETIENNE ANTHONY GIBBS
Executive & Group Development
P.O. Box 1303
St. Thomas, VI 00801-1303
(809) 774-4799 ● (809) 776-1927

Etienne Anthony Gibbs, MSW

Etienna Anthony Gibbs is a dynamic public speaker, trainer, and personnel management consultant. Born on the island of St. Thomas, U.S. Virgin Islands on December 31, 1946, Etienne has returned recently to his tropical hometown of Charlotte Amalie after 18 years of traveling, training, and teaching.

Etienne enlisted into the Air Force in 1969. He achieved his Bachelor of Arts degree in Sociology/Psychology from Chapman College, California in 1972. Upon completion of his four-year commitment to the Air Force, he earned a Masters of Social Work degree at Cal. State University, Sacramento in 1975. He then returned to the Air Force with a commission as First Lieutenant where he was assigned to the USAF Medical Center, Scott Air Force Base's Mental Health Clinic. Etienne soon became involved in the training of Red Cross volunteers to work with hospitalized patients and their families; training doctors, nurses, clergy and paraprofessionals to work with dying patients; and in training military and civilian Air Force supervisors in various aspects of counseling and referring.

In 1979, Etienne was transferred to the USAF Hospital in Wiesbaden, West Germany, where he provided indirect services to the released Iranian hostages. Captain Gibbs voluntarily separated from the Air Force in June, 1982, returning home with his German wife, Gisela. He plans to continue with his public speaking, training, personnel management consulting and writing activities.

HOW TO MOTIVATE YOURSELF WHEN OBSTACLES KNOCK YOU DOWN OR MAKING OBSTACLES WORK FOR YOU

by Etienne Anthony Gibbs, MSW

"Success is complete when you make your obstacles obsolete."

—Clarice O. Lindo

As a practicing psychotherapist assigned to various mental health clinics in the past years, I have worked with thousands of individuals, couples and families who have turned their obstacles into successes. The interesting thing is that, in spite of sometimes having difficulty expressing it, each person knew within himself exactly what he wanted to achieve and what course he was willing to take or reject. Each and every person has the ability to achieve his goals regardless of the number of obstacles in his way, but first he must learn to *motivate himself.*

Through a cumulation of personal, educational, and professional experiences, I have come to realize that obstacles in a person's life can become stepping stones to success. "How," you say, "can obstacles in my life become stepping stones to my success?" My answer is this: Using obstacles as an educational process to avoid problems of a similar nature in the future, a person can achieve any degree of success once he sets his mind to do so. In other words, once a person becomes *motivated* to achieve his goals, he puts himself in a position to benefit from his share of life's obstacles.

Before we go any further, let's arrive at a mutual understanding of the term "obstacles." According to the Webster dictionary, it is defined as "plural form for that which stands in the way, or opposes; a hindrance; an impediment; an obstruction." More specifically, the "obstacles" to which I refer are those everyday stress-inducing problems which affect each and every human being. These problems include marital/family conflicts; alcohol/drug abuse; separation/loss; terminal illness and suicide of loved ones; depression; and many other problems which prevent or impede our productive behavior.

Successful at Failing

It does not take much in order to understand how these stress-inducing problems impede productive activities in our occupational and domestic lives. We have been taught throughout our lives that obstacles stop us from reaching our goals. So, upon encountering the first obstacle, we immediately give up. This maladaptive pattern of behavior is guaranteed to lead us to failure. And some people teach themselves to become successful at failing. This failing behavior (both thinking it and doing it) substantiates the self-fulfilling prophecy countless times: "Problems (obstacles) mean I cannot succeed. Therefore, I will not succeed."

Let's glean an understanding of how these stress-inducing problems and maladaptive patterns of behavior affect us. As with anything else in life, these problems do not happen overnight. They run a slow and arduous course, presenting early warning signs along the way. I am primarily referring to the internal warning signs which we can learn to control. Some external factors can be controlled, others we cannot.

Stress is the one factor that may be produced internally and externally at the same time. While stress precipitated by external factors may not always be controlled by us, we definitely can control the stress precipitated by our internal factors, the stress precipitated by our maladaptive pattern of thinking and acting. Another way of looking at it: internal stress has early warning signs which we can control; while external stress may not always provide early warning signs. Therefore, by learning to refocus our thinking and behaving, we can reduce and ultimately eliminate internal stress, or obstacles. By learning to accept the things we cannot change, we are teaching ourselves an effective coping skill, an essential factor for maximal survival. By becoming alert to our internal and external stresses, we are beginning to motivate ourselves to overcome our obstacles.

Three Steps to Overcome Obstacles

To grapple with this ever-present problem, namely, motivating yourself to overcome obstacles, follow this three-step approach:

1. Become alert to your external and internal reaction to stress-inducing problems. Watch for early warning signs. These are indicated by any significant changes in your productive thinking and behaving.
2. Explore a plan of attack or course of action to reduce or eliminate future problems of a similar nature.
3. Activate that plan of attack or course of action immediately.

No two people experience the same types of obstacles, but everyone experiences common factors. Let's examine these common factors and the effects obstacles have upon our productive behavior or ultimate success.

In order to have a productive and healthy life, biological needs must be satisfied. All human beings need food for energy and sustenance; elimination of excess for maximal functioning; and rest, relaxation and sleep for recovery from exhausted energy.

Obstacles interfere with the input from basic energy sources, or with the output of energy or with both. For example, a person who keeps pushing himself on the job, working a record-setting period of fifteen hours daily for three or four weeks nonstop, will eventually become incapacitated or dysfunctional simply due to exhaustion.

In the USA workaholics from all walks of life visit doctors by the tens of thousands annually with this complaint.

Early Warning

So, in the case of the workaholic, he must become alert to his body's early warning signs: becoming easily irritable without just cause; becoming easily tired yet having difficulty sleeping; or becoming delusioned about his work habits and performance while his friends, loved ones, and significant others are beginning to notice a deterioration of his physical and mental functioning.

Evaluate your day-to-day functioning and your interaction with your friends, colleagues and family. If you receive unsolicitated objective feedback from these people that your physical and mental functioning is beginning to deteriorate, then you are lucky that your warning sign or obstacle has been identified so that you can turn it into a productive outcome.

If you find yourself to be such a high-strung workaholic, then, after identifying your traits, don't attempt to bring about sudden drastic changes in your behavior or personality. Human nature is such that the more you try to change, the more you'll fail. Instead, starting with small tasks, begin to formulate a corrective plan for yourself. For example, you might start by giving yourself ten or fifteen minutes in the morning, afternoon, and again in the evening for "My Quiet Time"—an adult version of the kindergarten's essential activity—"My Nap Time." Even if you do not nap, at least allow yourself to be free of all distractions, interruptions and annoyances. Many people utilize their rest, relaxation and sleep time in various productive ways. What's vitally important is to experiment and immediately activate a plan that works best for you.

A variation on the same theme is to set limits: allow yourself to work at your high-strung pace for short periods only. Interrupt a one or two-week high-strung pace with several days of rest, recreation, relaxation and sleep.

The nature of the obstacle, itself, does not matter; the end results are the same. If you allow obstacles to crowd your life, then you will deteriorate eventually to the point of helplessness, hopelessness and perhaps self-destruction.

So, let's look, in review, at how you can motivate yourself when obstacles knock you down.

Understanding Yourself, Your Habits and Your Environment

First, you must accept the premise that you are powerful and capable of turning your obstacles into a successful pattern. You might remember the old adage: "The operation was a success, but the patient died." So, too, it is for all of us in our daily lives. If we do not believe truly that we can pull ourselves through the most difficult obstacles, then the only thing at which we will succeed is failure. If we set for ourselves a pattern of maladaptive or self-deteriorating behavior, then we will succeed at becoming failures.

By paying particular attention to yourself, your habits, and your environment, you can learn to train yourself to glean the best of these areas. In your daily self-assessment, ask yourself:

A. How am I developing a healthy attitude, a winning attitude about myself?

B. Am I developing productive habits and benefiting from my mistakes and obstacles? What is my potential? Am I encouraging myself to develop and grow to my maximum potential? Am I satisfied with where I am? What am I going to do about it?

C. Am I satisfied with my geographic space at home and at work? What am I doing about it? What do I want to do about it? What space(s) do I use for rest, recreation, relaxation and sleep? Where and how do I divide my periods of rest, recreation, relaxation and sleep? Whom do I enclose in my personal space as friend, loved one and/or significant other? Am I satisfied with it as it is? What do I want to do about it?

Identifying and Understanding Your Obstacles

Once you can accept the premise that you can turn your obstacles into success, the next step is to identify and understand your obstacles. Do you have any control over them? Are you in a position to prevent them in the future? Are you creating your own obstacles? Are they caused by insufficient input (poor eating and sleeping habits); insufficient output (poor bodily functions and work performance caused by illness, laziness, or maladaptive patterns of behavior); or inappropriate integration with your environment (poor or lack of rest, recreation and/or work habits)?

In addition to giving yourself a routine 2000-mile check-up, have someone you trust give you an objective review of your behavior in different settings. Have him look particularly for your self-deteriorating traits.

Converting Your Negative Energy or Making Positive Choices

Now that you've assessed your self-deteriorating or maladaptive pattern of behavior, what are you going to do with it? Be sure to ask yourself: How much negative energy do I expend hourly, daily, or weekly, etc.? The energy that you used in trying to find ways to get back at your ex-wife/ex-husband, boss, parent-in-law and others could be put to better use. Once you understand and realize that a particular person or thing tends to trigger your anger button, why give that person or thing power over your life? Wouldn't it be better for you in the long run to minimize your interaction with that person or thing? It is okay, in fact, it is extremely healthy to express your anger. However, when this anger constantly creates obstacles in your life, it is time to look seriously at the early warning signs of your self-deteriorating behavior.

Activate and Maintain a Plan that Works Best for You

Then, in the final analysis, what course of action should you take? To recommend the most effective course of action on a collective basis is not only impossible, but it is also counterproductive, self-deteriorating behavior. Attempting to do so, I would be overstepping my limitations. I would be setting myself up for failure by biting off more than I can chew, more than I process. To do so, I would be setting an unrealistic goal since each and every individual is unique and responds best to his own care and management.

A key factor in creating, activating and maintaining your own effective plan lies in the following advice: Don't set yourself up for failure (don't create obstacles for yourself) by biting off more than you can chew or by setting unrealistic goals. There is no readily available individualized formula. However, modifying the following formula to your personal life circumstances, you can arrive at a plan that would be effective for you:

SI → SO + AIE → AEWS → MACs + ACA = $ucce$$

Sufficient **I**nput (food, rest, sleep)
   leads to:
      Sufficient **O**utput (Energy)
       plus
         Appropriate **I**ntegration with **E**nvironment
         (persons, places, things)
            leads to:
               Attention to **E**arly **W**arning **S**igns
               (Stress-inducing problems)
                  leads to:
                     Making **A**ppropriate **C**hoices
                     (Formulate a plan)
                      plus
                        Activation of a
                        Course of **A**ction
                        (Do it immediately.)
                        equals
                        $ucce$$

To motivate yourself, first become your own best friend.

MEMBER
NATIONAL SPEAKERS ASSOCIATION

SHANNON S. BARNETT
CIC Cosmetics International Corp.
8615 Inwood Road
Dallas, Texas 75209
(214) 271-5575 • (214) 358-4823

Shannon S. Barnett

Sales and marketing executive, editor, columnist, mother and speaker, Shannon S. Barnett is Director of National Expansion for CIC Cosmetics International Corporation in Dallas, Texas. CIC is one of the largest multilevel marketing cosmetic companies in the Southwest.

A human resource engineer with an educational background in Guidance and Counseling, her motivational speeches across the U.S. motivate audiences to mimic the overachiever with her witty, Texas-style wisdom.

She is author of Try Living With Overachievers . . . It Ain't Easy. *Her articles have appeared in many sales and feature magazines. She has been interviewed by newspaper writers and television personalities and is frequently profiled in national sales and marketing journals.*

TO MOTIVATE: CONCENTRATE!

(Or: How To Rob Overachievers of Their Number One Asset!)

by Shannon S. Barnett

"Before I was a genius, I was a drudge!"

—Paderewski

It happened to Vicky McClendon just as she was promoted to a regional district managerial position in her company. Her mother died. Then, as if her life had suddenly been put on an assembly line of catastrophe, there was more. Her seven-year-old son was hit by a car, underwent surgery and months of hospitalization. Her sister was diagnosed for cancer. On the few days she managed to make it into the office, Vicky stood at the large window behind her executive desk for most of her ten-hour-long workdays. She was completely unable to concentrate. All she could manage was "What's coming next?"

All of us have experienced times in our lives when fate seems to be handing out a double dose of bad news. Money has been tighter than tight. Our children have developed problems. Our marriages have been on the rocks, maybe even broken up. The nation, the economy, the spirit of our world depresses us every time we read the newspaper or listen to the news. We shake our heads, maybe get into a few emotionally heated discussions and then retreat back into our own worlds, our homes and our work. Sometimes we are able to make the problems help our concentration, as we plunge into our work as the only means of escape.

But when things get really bad, we can no longer really concentrate. And for many people, that's when the years of hard dedicated work start crumbling away.

What do you do when tragedy strikes at the summit of your career or as you are beginning it, running in high gear?

Is it normal to feel overloaded once in awhile, as if there are too many circuits pulling on you, demanding power? Can you ever pull the plug just temporarily without exploding everything you've nurtured and worked so hard for?

Time To Take Time Off

I have found through research that it is better to back away from your work whenever you feel this way. Psychologists claim that an overload of tragedy can lead to burnout, a psychological condition where employees may not be able to continue working. Burnout can be as serious as a nervous breakdown. I am not suggesting that you must take time off every three weeks or so. In fact, if you ever find that you have to request a leave of absence more than three times during your entire career, this may be indicative of another problem: the wrong profession. Unless the circumstances of your life warrant it, too much time off may mean you have a deeply rooted unhappiness with your present job. That's when it's time to find alternatives. We've all heard of the successful business executives who seem to vanish from behind the desk overnight. They leave successful careers, lovely families and run off to "find themselves" in the Virgin Islands or somewhere. If they had stopped to examine their feelings long before the overload hit, they could have changed their occupations before it was too late.

When cumulative tragedy strikes, time off provides a needed breather, a chance to flush your mind of whatever presently clogs it. Time off can provide the release that's needed to get you back into a state of mind where you can, once again, concentrate.

Concentration: It Takes Discipline

In the sales world, we often hear terms like "close," "prospecting," "goal setting," and "referrals." We commit them to memory and spend every spare moment studying them, polishing our closing techniques, reading up on new ways to market our products. But how many times do we read about ways to improve our concentration? We often fail to understand that concentration is the basis for everything. You can have the greatest techniques in the world, but if you're unable to concentrate, you'll never be able to give those techniques much justice.

First: **You Concentrate**

First, before doing anything else, you concentrate. What's so important about all this jargon on concentrating? It's never spelled out, but it is the basis, the underlying theme of most sales. Learn your business: that means, *concentrate on it.* Set goals, then *concentrate.* Follow through ... that means *concentrate* on the final objective.

Many times you'll hear people say the key to success is setting realistic, attainable objectives, then organizing your work so you can meet them. Yet enormously successful people seem to set goals beyond the realistic—goals that defy the odds of probability. There are hundreds of companies in the world today that are living proof that a wild card dream can become a reality. Listen to these people. They'll tell you all it took was hard work. But they won't tell you that beneath the hard work and sacrifice is a strong discipline called *concentration.* They won't tell you that, but not because it's a great, dark secret. To them, it's as natural as getting up in the morning.

I can hear the skepticism. I know what you're thinking because I've thought it too. You are thinking these successful people, these overachievers, have so much more than you do. They probably have brains, for one (and you're telling yourself you don't have brains) and maybe money. Money they either made or inherited. Then you'll tell me they have unusual talents. They are attractive people, they are not afraid to speak to strangers, get up in front of groups of two thousand, or two hundred. I know, you say you are sometimes so timid you can't even order a pizza because you're afraid of the pizza man. They had breaks, these overachievers. Breaks and luck. God was just on their side. No wonder they can concentrate. Right? Wrong!

Super People

Do you know what I mean when I talk about over-achievers—people who climb the ladder of life two or three rungs at a time, while we crawl up it slower than a tortoise? Once in awhile we get stuck on a rung that crashes in and takes us right down to the bottom and we start all over again. Overachievers, these super people who've got it made, are not affected by the tough times— things like divorce and accidents and bankruptcy. Life appears to go so smoothly for them we can only assume the overachiever, who has never crashed, has a special pact with the devil.

Let me tell you something. They don't. I have watched overachievers for years. I have watched them eat, sleep and drink; watched them balance their checkbooks, blow their noses (yes, they do that) and blow their horns. They even bleed when cut, just like the rest of us. I have, quite by accident, made it my life's ambition to analyze overachievers. Now that I'm almost through, I want to share my observations (so I can get on with other things).

The reason I know so much about this breed is that I was raised in a houseful of overachievers. We didn't need hot air in our carnival balloons to keep them up. We didn't need to hang pictures on the wall with nails. The air in our house was constantly moving because these overachievers were so busy rushing around doing everything. Didn't need a vacuum cleaner because the dust never did have time to settle.

At present, two members of my dear family are in *Who's Who In America.* One is listed in *Who's Who Of The Southwest.* As I was growing up, I really used to wonder what the difference was. While they were appearing in *Who's Who,* I already seemed to be president of "Who's Through."

Try Living With Overachievers!

Try, just try living with overachievers. It ain't easy. I was the first and only daughter in the family. In the South, we blonde-haired, blue-eyed daughters have it rough. We are supposed to keep the home fires burning. I tried to tell my parents that Atlanta burned a hundred years ago and they've rebuilt it sixteen times since, but they just smiled and brought in yet another teacher for another lesson. The women of the South are working overtime to shed this image. I'm glad. I've yet to meet a Southern gal who has time to curl her hair, sew her own frocks and sip Mint Juleps on the veranda. Shoot, most of us are up with the birds, stirring the home fires like the mammies used to long ago. It's the day-care dawdle: if you don't eat your breakfast and get dressed, young man and young lady, so I can get to the office, I'm going to start a fire under your bottom!

Given: I was expected to generally do nothing. Given:

everyone else around me was doing something. I ended up watching everything these overachievers were doing. I took notes. I learned some interesting things.

1. Overachievers seem to affect us in one of two ways. Either they intimidate us to the point that we quit trying and lie dormant, or there is awakened in us a righteous indignation that arms itself with a secret force. When we are pricked and stung, we respond. I call this the whiplash of necessity. You don't need to have this one X-rayed to know you've got it.

2. Overachievers truly do work hard. Very hard. Excruciatingly hard. They hardly ever eat. If they're overweight, they eat while they work and never think of it as eating. Most are not, however, overweight. Overachievers cannot stand *not* doing something creative, or constructive. H. Ross Perot, a noted Dallas millionaire and philanthropist, brown bags it for lunch, I'm told. No martinis for this man. He says his time is too valuable to waste it jabbering over three-hour lunches. He times himself for everything. He eats at his desk, watching his millions turn into billions.

3. Even if they are born with silver, gold or platinum spoons in their mouths, overachievers do not sky-rocket into success without hard work, and . . . concentration!

4. The overachiever runs in the fast lane with eyes wide open and does not avoid or hurdle the obstacles. He attacks them! He is actually very aware of what is happening all around him. Accumulating facts is his

second nature. Facts seem to motivate motivators even more.

5. When you hang around overachievers long enough, you no longer need to take vitamins or drink coffee. They have so much enthusiasm and energy it seeps into others. No more vitamin E.

6. The overachiever has to have his hands in everything. He is never the spectator but always a participant. Instead of reacting to happenings, the overachiever makes things happen.

In doubt? Let's go back to those earlier thoughts when we made up excuses as to why we haven't done anything with our lives.

What You've Got Is Everything!

"Overachievers," we said, "have brains and we don't." Well, that's just not true. I've known overachievers with average IQ levels, even below average IQ levels, who wowed everyone. There are a lot of smart people in the world today but brains can sometimes be a hindrance to success because they can make you lazy.

Money. That's right, overachievers have money. It came from somewhere, manna from heaven or a rich uncle or Mom. Just maybe, these people worked hard for the money they have? By hard I mean 18-20 hours a day.

Talent. Overachievers are born with natural talents. Nonsense. Ever wonder why entertainers and actresses can screw up their lives so marvelously? They are certainly born with vast amounts of talent. Yet few make it to the top. Even if they do, it's usually not without problems and heartbreaks.

Start Your Own Network!

Speaking of heartbreaks, we said we were different from overachievers in that the overachiever seems to get special breaks out of life. Right time at the right place. Ever wonder why that doesn't happen to you? Could it be that you are never anyplace where something can happen to you? It's amazing what happens when people start networking, meeting other professionals, and sharing ideas and creativity. They learn and grow. Then the rest of the world looks at them bitterly and says, gee, they had to know someone; they had a connection. Sure they knew someone, they make it their business to know a lot of people!

Fact: Overachievers make connections. They bird-dog. Successful free-lance writers I know don't go to bed at night until they've written one or two idea letters to a national magazine. Successful business people aren't afraid to call and contact someone in another company they've heard of and would like to meet. Nothing wrong with getting a mentor, either. So you've always admired Henry Kissinger? Next time he's in town, go listen to him speak. Sit down and write the man a letter!

How many times have we been frustrated because we see another person, an overachiever, doing a job we feel is very easy—a job we feel capable of doing. I often watch young executives go through extreme mental torture because they believe they are ready to become managers. They can't understand why they haven't been offered a job. After all, what's so hard about sitting behind a big desk, signing documents, entertaining guests, taking three-hour lunches, et cetera?

What they don't know, or don't see, is the getting there. To be, we must all first become. I was amused by a young high school boy who told me the other day what he wanted to be when he grew up: a manager. I gently asked him if he thought he could maybe start as a salesman and work his way up. He thought about it carefully and said, "No, I like to guide people." "How then, would you guide them if you don't know what they do?" I asked. The boy just didn't know.

Fact: Overachievers wear invisible blinders. They don't care about office politics. They just care about getting ahead.

If you think I've sort of switched sides, you're right! I want to beat the overachiever at his own game. If I cross sides in the process, well, fine. It's quite simple. The overachiever overdoes everything. He forgets the necessary work and becomes an *over* do-er. Do what's necessary, then do some more. The way I see it. the only way to beat this breed of humanity is to bluff them by joining their game plan. Believe me, it ain't easy living with overachievers. It's just a lot easier to become one.

Shannon's steps to overachieving:

1. Start to *concentrate* now.
2. Get a special place in your home or office where you start off everything you do at a certain time (I like morning) by concentrating on what it is you're going to accomplish. Make a mental outline in your head.

Take it step by step.

3. Once you establish the physical place, make it a point to *sit there for a full 21 days straight,* including weekends. Now do 20 minutes of uninterrupted work. No phone calls. If not answering the phone worries you, get an answering machine so you can screen calls. Or tell your secretary, "Emergency calls only." Every "little second" someone takes will subtract time from your concentration, from your achievements.

4. Remember the deciding edge lies with learning the basics, executing them, and practicing, networking, practicing.

5. Have a love affair with your career. If this is impossible, maybe it's time for a change. There are ample opportunities in the world today for self-employment. Remember, all it takes is action after you concentrate on it!

No one is born a success. It takes hard work. Success is evolutionary, not revolutionary. Once you've faced these facts, the overachievers in your life won't bother you, they'll challenge you on to greater and greater goals. This is how I learned to play their game . . . and best of all, this is how I learned to win. And guess what . . . you can do it too!

No one can make you feel inferior without your consent.

—Eleanor Roosevelt.

BILL STEVENS
Timberlake Stevens Association
4059 South 99th Street
Greenfield, WI 53228
(414) 321-9555 • (414) 545-3381

Bill Stevens

Bill Stevens is President of Timerlake Stevens Associates, a business seminar and consulting company he started nine years ago, and TSA Business Brokers in Milwaukee, Wisconsin.

In addition to his entrepreneurial pursuits, Bill presents speeches, workshops and seminars for trade associations, hospitals, business and educational organizations from coast to coast. His seminars include Listening, the Quiet Skill; Management Burnout: Signs, Symptoms, Causes and Cures; How to Negotiate Any Problem, Without Anyone Losing; *and others.*

He specializes in helping organizations develop management talent through training, goal setting and regular feedback. He is also a consultant "catalyst," helping managers and executives find win-win solutions to internal and external problems, and in developing management and work teams.

Prior to founding his own firm in 1974, he held management positions with American Can Company, Celanese Corporation, and Chicago and Northwestern Railroad. Bill earned an MBA degree from New York University and has authored several articles on Burnout and Management in several professional journals.

HAVE YOU MOTIVATED YOURSELF TO BURN OUT?

by Bill Stevens

"Love is perhaps a process of my leading you gently back to yourself."

—**Saint Exupary**

Burnout

Burnout: "When your emotional center caves in and you have nothing left to give."

Did you ever wake up in the morning, unable to sleep any longer, and unable to get up? You lie there for a few minutes, trying to remember why you woke up in the first place, and what it is you are supposed to do today. "Oh, that's right," you think. "The office. I have to go to the office. To heck with it. I'll call in sick. Why can't I get sick like other people do?"

Then one by one, you count off the important meetings. Besides, if you miss today, you'll have twice as much to do tomorrow. And the next day, and the next day. It will never go away. You throw off the covers, and the day has begun. You hope as you jump into the shower that maybe the splashing water will wash the heaviness away. Your old vital, energetic, smiling self will once more emerge. But what leaves the house instead is a grim, unsmiling figure. A little bent, a little tired, lips and shoulders set to get the day's work done.

In this frame of mind, the day will surely be irritating. There will be too much work, too many interruptions, too many details, too few rewards. You may find yourself yelling at your staff and even being short with your customers. The whole day will probably be marked by fatigue and tension. Even its ending will not bring exhilaration, because the problem is not just work. Even your family, friends and associates have become flat and stale. Now that you have what you want, you wonder why you ever wanted it in the first place.

If you can put yourself in this picture, you may be burned out. If so, you aren't alone. According to psychologists, burnout is common among nurses, doctors, dentists, police, social workers, managers and executives and other professionals who are so busy helping other people, they often neglect their own needs.

This chapter will guide you through the various signs and symptoms of burnout so you know what to watch out for. It will also show you how you set yourself up for burnout. Finally, it will present you with a "table-full" of solutions that you can choose from to minimize the chances of your burning out.

What To Watch For:
The Signs and Symptoms of Burnout

There are many signs of impending burnout. Those we

have listed below happen to everybody at some time or another. Feeling fatigue, for example, does not mean you are burned out. If, however, you find you are feeling an unusual degree of three or more of the following symptoms, you may be at the first stage of burnout.

Physical Signs and Symptoms

Fatigue. You are aware of a chronic tiredness that never seems to leave you. The things you usually do to get over it just don't work. You take the weekend off, but still have to drag yourself back to the office on Monday.

Aches and Pains. You may have trouble with lower back pain, or have more headaches, upset stomach or even ulcers. You feel a general stiffness and tightness throughout your body.

Increased Self-Medication. You find yourself taking more drugs and medicines in an effort to get some relief.

Performance Signs and Symptoms

Inability to make decisions. You wish you didn't have to decide anything. Even deciding where to go for lunch seems to be overwhelming. You try to avoid deciding anything and may therefore feel immobilized.

Working Harder To Keep Up. Maybe if you push harder, you can catch up and get some relief. Instead, it just makes it worse.

Boredom and Low Motivation. Nothing is "happening" for you. Your job isn't "fun" any more. It seems you are doing the same things over and over and getting nothing from them.

Increased Time Away From The Office. You need more days off. You often find yourself running late for meetings. Maybe you forget one or two appointments. You are mentally absent—just not plugged in.

Accident Proneness. Because you are not as aware of your physical surroundings, you bump into chairs and tables or step on your dance partner's toes more often than usual. You may become involved in an automobile accident or at least have a few near misses.

Emotional Signs and Symptoms

Loss of Your Sense of Humor. Things just don't look funny for you any more. It's difficult to see humor in situations, especially when it's about you.

Worry. You find yourself doing an inordinate amount of worrying that something is going to happen. Something is going to happen to your job, your marriage, your health.

Feeling Trapped. You feel more controlled by your work and your family than fulfilled by it. There are too many have-to's. It feels like there is nothing you can do about your condition.

Feelings of Failure. Feeling that somehow you have failed yourself, or failed others. You are no longer able to distinguish between failure and a lack of success.

Guilt. Guilt about not spending enough time with your family or on all of the things that have to get done on your job. You aren't meeting your own expectations. No matter what you choose, you feel guilty.

Declining Self-image. You don't like being who you are right now. Not only do you not like what you see on the outside, but you don't like what you are on the inside.

Alienation. You don't like people very much right now, any more than they like you. So you cut off relationships, even those that could sustain you.

Cynicism and Griping. You find yourself doing more and more complaining and grousing to people about what is happening in your world.

Anger and Resentment. You do more blaming. You lose your cool a little more often. You feel resentful about how life is treating you.

Use the worksheet below to check off each of these symptoms you now feel. If three or four are on the high side, you might begin to look at how you may actually be setting yourself up. In fact, if you do, you will have taken the first step toward preventing serious burnout.

SIGNS AND SYMPTOMS OF BURNOUT

Tune into the here and now. For each of the signs and symptoms, indicate on the scale of 0-100 where you are right now. Use the scale regularly—once a week if you feel burnout coming on, or once a month to detect symptoms before they become a problem. Use it at staff meetings to monitor staff burnout.

Personal Signs and Symptoms

PHYSICAL

Fatigue	0 _____	100
Physical Symptoms	0 _____	100
Increased Self-Medication	0 _____	100

PERFORMANCE

Inability to Make Decisions	0 _____	100
Work Harder to Keep Up	0 _____	100
Boredom/Low Motivation	0 _____	100
Increased Absenteeism	0 _____	100
Accident Proneness	0 _____	100

EMOTIONAL

Loss of Sense of Humor	0 _____	100
Worry	0 _____	100
Feeling Trapped	0 _____	100
Failure	0 _____	100
Guilt	0 _____	100
Declining Self-Image	0 _____	100
Alienation	0 _____	100
Cynicism/Griping	0 _____	100
Anger/Resentment	0 _____	100

How You Can Cause Yourself To Burnout

The key to eliminating burnout is knowing exactly how you get yourself into burnout condition. There is a key word here. That word is *you*. In order to deal with *your* burnout, it's manditory that you begin to accept full responsibility for it. It's yours. It belongs to *you*.

As we go through the list of burnout sources, refer to the worksheet at the end of this section. Check off those that may apply to you. If it is one of your "biggies," use ++ as an indicator. If it is an occsaional "contributor," use +.

If it does not describe you, just leave it blank. Be as honest and objective as you can.

Choosing Not To Set Limits. When you don't recognize that you have physical, emotional and skill limitations, or if you won't say no, or if you try to do it all, you will burn out. Are you working sixty hours a week and serving on four committees you really don't want to be on? Are you trying to prove something to someone by trying to be super-executive, super-parent, super-friend all rolled into one? If you are, you are doing it unto yourself.

Choosing Not To Pay Attention To Your Own Wants and Needs. When you decide not to pay attention to what you want or need, your needs don't go away. Instead, those needs go unmet. They build up inside until they explode or burn a hole in your stomach. Pretending that your needs aren't important is like pretending that you aren't important.

Choosing Not To Communicate Your Feelings. Somewhere along the way in our society, we set up the unwritten rule that we should keep our feelings to ourselves. Maybe it is because we believe that others will not understand. They might laugh, or feel hurt or angry. When our feelings are rejected, we feel rejected.

If you have difficulty sharing your anger, frustration, fear, or even joy, you're vulnerable to burnout. As you save and collect your feelings, your stomach begins to keep count. Saving feelings is like saving trading stamps in a book. When we collect enough stamps, we can turn them in for free prizes. When we save up feelings, we do the same thing. The prizes? If you are a red (anger) stamp collector, you can turn them in for a free tantrum or a blowup. If you collect blue (hurt) stamps, you are entitled to a free sulk, or perhaps if you have saved for a long time, a free depression. The prize is your choice.

Choosing To Isolate Yourself Physically and Emotionally. Instead of finding others to talk to, some people choose to retreat into themselves. They believe they don't need anybody. Going away from people when you need them the most results in cutting off your supply of necessary energy that results from the nurturing and affirmation that we all need as humans. Do you tend to isolate yourself?

Choosing Not To Acknowledge Your Power. You and I are powerful people. We can change almost anything we want to change. We can do what we want to do. We can paint any scene we want to and step into it. Some accept and acknowledge that power. Others deny it. Check to see if you use the power that you were given at birth.

Choosing To Ignore Positive Attention From Others. It is difficult for some of us to accept compliments. It may be because we feel unworthy. It may be because we were taught to be humble and not brag. Ignoring the gift of a compliment or the attention someone gives us just because they want to give it is to deny ourselves this gift which we all need to prevent ourselves from burning out.

Choosing To Become Overinvolved. Being over-involved means being responsible *for* your family, friends and assocaites instead of being responsible *to* them. Many people take problems home with them. At least they do so in their heads. Others do things for people that they can and want to do for themselves, just so the doer can feel good. If you have not developed "detached caring," you may be courting burnout.

Choosing Not To Learn Communication Skills. Almost all of us have learned to use our language. But there is more to communicating than speaking it or writing it. Most of us have never learned to distinguish the true meaning behind the words, or the feelings that are being expressed. We haven't been taught how to listen, or to confront in positive ways.

Choosing To Be Unable To Live With The Grey Areas of Life. You have to check with others every time you want to make a move. You have to see everything in absolutes—in blacks and whites. You live by "shoulds" and "oughts." You have to make sure it is all right to "do it this way." You are also more likely to burn out if you choose not to pave your own way when there are no rules.

Worksheet for
Personal Sources of Burnout

1. Not setting limits _____

2. Not paying attention to my own needs and wants _____

3. Not communicating my feelings _____

4. Isolating myself physically and psychologically _____

5. Powerlessness _____

6. Ignoring positive attention from others _____

7. Becoming overinvolved _____

8. Lack of professional communication skills _____

9. Inability to live with the "grey areas" of life _____

Personal Strategies for Preventing Burnout

There is no one best way for everyone to prevent burnout or to minimize their susceptibility to burnout. Following are several strategies for you to choose from. Trust yourself to know which are the best for you. Select two or three strategies that you believe will work for you and that you are willing to try. Put two check marks next to those. If you find others that you believe might also work, put a single check next to those.

Physical Strategies

Exercise. _____
Find some form of exercise that is *enjoyable* to you and find some time to do it *every day.*

Nutrition _____
Eat balanced meals. More green beans and fewer French fries; more protein, fewer starches and sugars.

Relaxation _____
Whatever it is for you—meditation, music, quiet walks, reading, or a hot tub—do it as often as you can.

Relationship Strategies

Regular Contact
With A Peer Support System _____
Get together regularly with fellow professionals with whom you can share your frustrations, concerns and triumphs.

Re-examine Your Relationships _____
Take a look at whom you support and who supports you. Consider dropping relationships that don't add to your life.

Put Yourself First _____
You are the single most important person in your world. Be first while at the same time acknowledging others' firstness. Nobody has to be last.

Resolve Unresolved Conflicts _____
If you have long-standing conflicts with important others in your life, they are sapping your emotional energy. Get them resolved.

Skill Training Strategies

Human Communications Skills _____
Attend workshops or seminars on how to listen, how to confront, how to express feelings.

Assertiveness Training _____
Assertiveness is standing up for yourself, without it being at the expense of others.

Conflict Resolution Skills _____
Learn how to resolve conflicts so that everyone involved wins.

Time Management _____

If you are pressured by time and need help in managing that scarce commodity, take a time management seminar.

Strategies For Taking Care of Yourself

Increasing Your Awareness
of Yourself and Others _____

Begin to know yourself and what you think and feel, want and need. Be aware of what bothers you. Become aware of others. Take notice of them. Look into their eyes. Know your signs and symptoms.

Develop A Decompression Routine _____

Try a different route home tonight. Wear clothes that you feel good in. Sit in the office for another twenty minutes before you leave. Use a different routine.

Say No When You Mean No _____

Decide to stop doing things that you don't want to do. You have a right *not* to want to do something. Say yes only when you mean yes.

Take An I Love _____ Day _____

Fill your name in the blank and take a day just for yourself, to do anything you want to do. No responsibilities today. Just "want to's."

Take Notice of Positive
Statements Toward You _____

Look for compliments. Hear the positives. Take it in and let it warm you. If you can't think of anything to say, just say "Thanks."

Ask For What You Want And Need _____
Be honest about what you want. Let people know, so they can give it to you. Stop making others try to guess what you want.

Make A Want List _____
It can be a silly list or a sane list. Start thinking about goals, where you want to be, when and with whom.

Live In The Moment _____
The moment is all we have. Stop worrying about what you did a long time ago, or what others did to you. That can only blind you to the opportunities of the moment. Feel what is going on now and do something about it.

Deal With Your Anger _____
Anger is a normal human emotion. Learn how to express it in positive ways. Find out what emotion triggers your anger. Is it really fear? hurt? embarrassment?

Take Time And Space For Yourself _____
Take time that is just yours. Be with yourself.

Stop Living To Please Others _____
Others will decide whether they are pleased with you or not. It is up to them. Start living to please *you*.

Re-examine Your Values _____
If you find yourself wrapped up in value conflicts, take time to re-examine them. Where did they come from? What experiences have you had to reaffirm them? Let those values go that don't work for you, and hold on to those that do.

Stop Self-putdowns _____
Who needs them. Do it enough and you start believing

them. Substitute self-praise. You deserve it.

Acknowledge Responsibility
For Yourself

Feel the power that comes from knowing that you are in control. You decide your feelings and your thoughts. Give up blaming others.

Keep A Feelings Diary

If you don't find someone to share feelings with or don't feel comfortable doing it, write them down. It will give you the catharsis that you need.

This list is only a beginning. You know many other strategies for taking care of yourself. Remember, it is up to you. When things just don't feel right, take a look at your symptoms. If they are there, check what you are doing to yourself. Then, make the necessary changes to take care of yourself. That is the greatest gift that you can give to your family, your staff, your associates and all those who really care about you.

THOMAS L. KOZIOL

Thomas L. Koziol, Management Consultant
7597 Putman Road
Vacaville, CA 95688
(707) 446-1468

Thomas L. Koziol

Thomas L. Koziol wears three hats: consultant, speaker and author. He specializes in motivational and effective stress management training for all organizational levels.

In his consultant role, his message is that a positive motivational environment is possible through understanding self and others. His unique methods include self-report instrumentation, role playing, feedback, humor and personal experience.

He addresses the inner thoughts and feelings of all participants to stimulate action, because he believes the potential within people is unlimited.

In his speaker role, he urges the audience to reach out and achieve at the level at which they are most comfortable. Once there, scan the next plateau and go for it! His Effective Stress Management program presents the only stress identifier anyone will ever need to handle, cope and understand stress.

In his role as an author, he has written: The Job Interview Manual, Youth Assistance Program *and the* One Minute Exercise Kit.

His programs are professional, educational, memorable and refreshingly different.

HOW TO FIND THE MOTIVATIONAL HOT BUTTON
by Thomas L. Koziol

"If you believe you can't, you can't."

—Henry Ford

Mention the word motivation and almost immediately the names Maslow, Herzberg and McClelland come into mind. Move over gentlemen, because motivation according to Koziol may not replace your valuable work, but will certainly add a new dimension.

Of necessity, I will be flirting with the theories of these learned gentlemen because:

a) I, too, studied their works in school, and
b) have and am living and seeing their words being put into practice.

Positive Motivational Environment

I have come to the conclusion, after five years in the public relations field observing the successful as well as the not-so-successful, that the only motivation necessary to achieve whatever success you dream of is: *Self-motivation.* Motivation that comes from inside; a burning spark that aches to become a blaze.

My theory of motivation, called Positive Motivational Environment (PME), originates from the inner self. Achievement is geared to plateaus or comfort levels. I encourage people to—*Go for it!*—but at a comfortable pace, aiming efforts and channeling energies at goals that are attainable.

The motivational environment is like the weather: it varies by degrees and conditions. I demonstrate in my PME program how to create that atmosphere most conducive to achievement.

Three Statements

My belief about motivation centers around these three statements:
1. I cannot motivate you, but
2. you are motivated, and
3. you do things for your reasons and *not* mine.

I hope these statements do not sound radical. I am not a radical. I am a motivational and sales trainer who deals with people—people who have thoughts, perceptions and individual realities. All of these must not only be recognized but dealt with.

Hot vs. Cold Button

I believe that pressing the motivational *hot* button produces a more positive and productive reaction than pressing the *cold* button. The difference being, the hot button is the motivator, while the cold button is fear. I see the use of fear as being counterproductive and unnecessary.

I will articulate the complex process known as motivation, through its components. I believe these components are:
1. understanding self
2. understanding others.

I feel I can push the hot instead of the cold button(s) by better understanding self and others.

Motivational Continuum

There exists, on the motivational continuum, one or more motivating factors that will be common to both of us. In a given situation, what motivates you *will* motivate me. Also on the same continuum and existing to a larger degree, I believe, is the reality that what motivates you *will not* motivate me, and vice versa. This aspect must also be recognized and dealt with.

Premise, Goal, and Friction

If we accept that there are factors that are the same motivational-wise for both you and me, then that common situation must incorporate our needs, wants and desires. I believe this is the basis from which all attempts at motivation should start. If you know my goal and not only accept it into your sphere but include it as part of your goal(s), I will be successful. And, so will you.

If on the other hand, you do not perceive my goal as being totally in consonance with your goal(s), you will probably reject my goal. It is at this point that friction develops.

I can reduce and probably eliminate this friction if I have an understanding of both *you and me*. Understanding self and others needs to be considered.

Two Statements

Two statements about the underlying factors of motivation must now come into focus. They are:

1. If I understand you better than you understand me, I control the communication. (This principle has been known for years. Some of the most (in)famous leaders in history have applied it to acquire power and large chunks of real estate.)

2. If I understand you better than you understand yourself, I control *you!* (Again, some of these same men were able to go as far as they did because they understood their subordinates (nations?) better than the people understood themselves.)

Confusing? Not really. Remembering that I said I do things for my reason(s) and not yours, helps to clarify and understand these statements.

Clarification of Control

Sectionalizing both statements will help to uncloud what I mean.

Statement number one:

If I understand you . . . (This means I know you. I have an idea as to your hot and cold buttons.)
better than you understand me . . . (You may know me, but only superficially and do not have any idea as to *my* hot or cold buttons.)
I control the communication . . . (It stands to reason that if I know your hot and cold buttons but you do not know mine, I am in a position to better control the communication. I am in command of the situation.)

Statement number two:

If I understand you . . . (Same as statement number one.)
better than you understand yourself . . . (A slight twist here. Notice, I say *yourself* instead of *me*. This means that I not only understand me but I understand you better than you understand either one of us.)
I control you . . . (It follows that if I understand you better than you understand yourself, I *do* control you.)

Think of the consequences of these statements. I am in control in both situations so the picture is rosy from my side. It probably is very different, however, from your vantage point.

I believe that parity, or as near to parity as possible, must exist in order to have motivational effect.

Maslow Revisited

Before I move into the actual realm of motivation (where parity must exist), I will touch upon Maslow's hierarchy of needs. This theory seems to be the one with which most people are familiar and which they associate with motivation.

The first need Maslow suggests is physiological: hunger, thirst, etc.

Next comes safety: sense of security, safe from harm, etc.

Belonging is the next need: love, affection, etc., are examples.

Following belonging is esteem: acceptance of self and recognition by others.

The last need is self-actualization. This is the need to become all that you can become.

The theory suggests that a person satisfies one need before attempting to satisfy the next need in the hierarchy.

I believe that as participants in this all-too-real game known as life, we do not graduate from one need to the next and stay there, but constantly flow up and down the needs hierarchy according to the situation at hand.

Two Examples

When I was sky diving, my need for self-actualization was met only when I landed, in one piece, and could get up and walk away. While preparing to jump from the airplane, I not only had to anticipate my physiological and safety needs, but I had to concentrate on them exclusively. Failing that, I would not have to worry about self-actualization. Hence, the motivational environment at the sky diving center was heavy on safety and physiological needs enhancement and light on self-actualization. After the jump, the needs were reversed. Self-actualization became primary because I was down and could then relate my experience to my expectations.

I believe we follow the same pattern in our business, work, social and home lives. As an example, take the employee who is about to be evicted from his apartment. What need do you think he is concentrating upon?

You may not, for one reason or another, be aware of the circumstances, so you make the erroneous assumption that the employee no longer cares about his work or the company. After all, the behavior you observed shows him tardy in the morning, taking protracted lunch hours and leaving early. Unless you take steps to ascertain the actual reason for this nonacceptable performance, you will proceed with your uninformed assessment. If you opt to fire the person, you will be addressing a totally incorrect need for both the employee and you. That would be tragic for both parties.

This point of traversing the hierarchy of needs, therefore, must be a consideration in the motivational environment.

Understanding of Self and Others.

The process of understanding self and others will be best explained, I believe, by viewing it through its components. They are:

1. the communication process
2. goal setting
3. stress

The Communication Process (four parts) . . .

1. speaking
2. listening
3. writing
4. reading.

Speaking and listening constitute the lion's share of communication—30 and 45 percent respectively, according to studies done at Ohio State University. While writing and reading comprise the remaining 25 percent, they are only message vehicles (at least as I see them). If the motivational environment is not positive, these vehicles will be totally ineffective because they will be ignored. Consider for example, the organization in which the boss is the "You will do it my way" type. The vehicles (writing and reading) will not be utilized at all. The workers will be tuned into listening.

I will address speaking and listening. Please note: listening and *not* speaking received the largest rating. The ability to listen effectively plays a major role in the understanding of self and others and consequently, in the arranging for a positive motivational environment. I believe that the effective listener is the effective motivator because the effective listener is probably the effective delegator. I will illustrate this point through two scenarios.

Scenario #1:

Boss behind paper-stacked desk working on three reports, answering two telephone lines, attempting to dictate a letter. Subordinates are sitting behind their desks writing personal letters, drinking coffee, waiting, etc.

Scenario #2:

Boss behind desk that has one or two reports. Flow chart on the wall (or maybe in the desk drawer) with the names of the subordinates followed by the title of the project and suspense and in-phase check date blocks filled in. Subordinates are working on their assignments both in and out of office.

I think you will agree with me that scenario number two is the type of situation to be working in because the boss knows how to delegate.

Effective delegators (listeners) know their limitations (cannot do it all) and instead of taking these limitations as personal affronts, use their subordinates to compensate in those areas. Through these delegator-actions, the subordinates are given an opportunity to flex their muscles (skills) and to learn and grow. If subordinates make mistakes, the effective listeners (delegators) will help "fix" the mistakes, and keep the project on track.

I believe the employees in scenario number one would be chastised for any and all mistakes and, in time, would give up completely. The absence of motivation has a striking impact.

Walk and Talk

In looking at the basic question,

"How did the effective listener become an effective listener?"

the answer is, this person . . .

1. employs the walk-and-talk policy
2. lets others have their say
3. does not prejudge either the people or the task.

The walk-and-talk policy has the boss getting out from behind the desk and walking (or driving) to the various work centers under his control and talking to the "working troops." Studies have shown that the chief executive officer (substitute manager, foreman, supervisor, etc.) who leaves the confines of his office for an occasional visit with the work force, will see far more productivity than the chief executive officer who sits in his office and sends orders and paperwork in his place. I view the walk-and-talk policy as the eyes and ears of the boss. He sees and hears, firsthand, what the rank-and-file perceive as the company's policies, goals, etc. This walk-and-talk policy has a additional benefit:

The workers feel that their positions and con-tributions are important.

If practiced on an ongoing basis, credibility of the communication process is strengthened in the organization. That is, when the workers receive a message, whether written or verbal, they will believe it; this results in making the delegating process easier. Resistance to acceptance of a delegated task will be practically non-existent.

Lets Others Have Their Say

The second important step in becoming an effective listener is the ability to let others have their say without interfering. I often find myself wanting to jump right in and talk. The speaker may be using emotional verbage or clouding the issue so I feel compelled to "straighten him out." If I let the speaker get it all out, I discover that I am better able, not only to assess the situation, but to take the appropriate action.

Does Not Prejudge Either the People or the Task

Another attribute of an effective listener is an open mind. I know that if I do not prejudge the situation or person, I am more effective. Having a person tell me about a situation I have not seen, for example, allows me ample opportunity to prejudge that situation. If I wait until I am on scene and make my own observations, I can handle the situation with objectivity.

Goal Setting

I cannot conceive of a motivational environment devoid of goals. As I mentioned under the Motivational Continuum, if you know my goal and incorporate it into your sphere, we both will be successful. I believe goal setting and goal explanation to be as necessary as effective communication in the setting of a positive motivational environment. Obviously, it is through communication that we make our goals known. Acceptance or rejection of same is also made known through communications. Hence, I must be able to tell you exactly what I mean regarding my expectations of and for both of us.

I am of the opinion that a goal must be specific, detailed and measurable. Saying something like:
"I want to increase production by 20 percent"
is nice, but it does not mean anything. Increase production of what by when? By whom? A better statement would be:
"I want to increase production of the dye room by 20

percent no later than July of this year with the current dye room staff."

The foreman of the dye room, at minimum, would be in attendance at the meeting in which this goal was established. I would want his input as to whether or not my standard was reasonable, fair and within the capacity of the dye room to accomplish. Failure to include anyone from the dye room would most assuredly result in a quick demise of my goal. The work center must include my goal into their goal.

I recommend that goal setting be undertaken in a less than grandiose (a lot of shouting, flash, pomp, hysteria, etc.) method.

First, make the parts of the goal attainable. That is, segment the goal into achievable sections. Do not set the requirements at such a level that they are impossible to reach. If you do, frustration sets in and your goal goes by the wayside.

Next, make the sections measurable by time, quantity, quality, or whatever parameter is appropriate.

Then, follow up. Check to see the progress on the path to attainment. Utilize the walk-and-talk policy and give positive feedback and positive strokes. I guarantee this will practically insure goal achievement. After completion, reward those who helped in the process.

I have presented a fractionalized portion of the three components of understanding self and others because each area is a volume unto itself, yet interconnected. These areas, along with stress, constitute the base of the launching pad for a positive motivational environment. I will tie these points into a neat bow after I discuss stress.

Stress

Stress is "the" buzzword for the 80s. Hardly a day goes by where some expert or another isn't on television relating how to recognize and combat stress. I, too, believe stress must be recognized and dealt with in a manner satisfactory to all concerned parties.

I define stress as a pressure (outside forces) plus tension (inner feelings).

Pressure, or outside forces, consists of demands and change. Demands made by supervisors, spouses, friends, relatives, job perceptions, economic conditions, etc. Change comes in the form of a new job, promotion, demotion, pay cut, pay raise, birth, death, etc.

Tension, or inner feelings, are such sensations as the knotted stomach, headache, backache, etc.

Both pressure and tension vary as to degree, by situation. Referring back to scenario one, the boss probably felt a lot of pressure and tension while the boss in scenario two, felt little of either. Boss number two did have stress because he still was *responsible* for the work, no matter who was doing it. He managed to keep stress under control by using several of the many tools available. Boss number one could have used the same tools but selected to ignore them. I find another method to be extremely useful in combating stress: relaxation.

When I find myself bordering on stress overload, I sit back, take a deep breath, assess the situation to see if I can leave it for a few minutes, and if I can, I go for a walk. I then concentrate on the walk and let the stress propel me until I can regain control. I know of others who shut the door, do not accept phone calls during this period, put their feet on the desk, and lie back in the chair. No matter what you find to be relaxing, *do it!* The alternatives (ulcers, heart problems, etc.) are not worth foregoing the time to relax.

Tieing It All Together

I believe I do things for my reasons and not yours and that the same holds true for you. If we never had to interact, this fact would be inconsequential. However, we do interact not only at work but socially. It is, therefore, important for both of us to be able to address each other on as equal a footing as possible. I see that the best possible means for achieving parity is through understanding: I understand you and you understand me. I minimize contact with your cold button (fear) while maximizing contact with your hot button (motivation) in this way. This increases the opportunity to have a positive motivational environment.

Understanding self and others is accomplished by gathering experience, being aware of the communication process and how it works in your organization, having concrete, measurable goals, and managing stress.

SELMA H. LAMKIN
Nikmal Publishing
698 River Street
Boston, MA 02126
(617) 361-2101

Mrs. Selma H. Lamkin, C.P.A.

A practicing accountant, author, and educator. Her expertise in the field of finance has won her recognition as a consultant of practical information on money and investments. She has been included in Who's Who of American Women, *the* International Who's Who, *and in the* Personalities of America. *She has been recently named in the* Who's Who in America Among Business and Professional Women *for her significant career achievements.*

Ms. Lamkin graduated from Bentley College of Accounting and Finance, as well as Hebrew Teachers College. Ms. Lamkin has written five books entitled: Money Management and Investment; Self-Instruction Accounting; Small Business Success Manual; Shoebox Syndrome or Record-Keeping *and* Do It Right the First Time—A Guide to Computer Installation.

She offers bookkeeping and tax services and preparation of financial statements for individuals and businesses.

She is the Treasurer of the Massachusetts Women's Political Caucus, Legislative Chair of the Fanuel Hall Business and Professional Women, and on the Steering Committee of the American Women in Federal Contracts. She is also a charter member of the Women's Athletic Club.

THE MOTIVATION OF MONEY
by Selma H. Lamkin

> *"Taxes are the price of civilization so why do we hate the price of civilization so much more than the price of automobiles? It is because with automobiles you get sort of what you pay for. Many people leave the price sticker in the window of their new car, proud of what they pay. Have you seen anyone leave or paste their income tax return on their window?"*

> **—Anonymous**

Secrets Your Tax Advisor Never Tells You

I'm going to share with you some little-known techniques for slashing your taxes. You'll never hear them from your tax advisor, unless you are married to one. And maybe not even then!

Is your tax advisor deliberately keeping secrets from you? Of course not. But let's face it: He or she has dozens—maybe hundreds—of clients. How much time does he/she really spend thinking about your unique, individual tax situation?

Your tax advisor is probably dealing with people on an assembly line basis. Knows they can keep you happy by throwing just one or two ideas your way, then, on to the next client.

To help you take advantage of the real tax breaks, your tax advisor must be totally familiar with your business or profession; has to know your relations with your family, your hobbies, your travel and entertainment patterns, your investment goals plus your personal habits. In short, everything you do.

That's a pretty tall order for a person you see a few times a year, possibly only once.

Unless you can afford the luxury of a full-time tax advisor, you will have to make up your mind to dig out the secrets of tax avoidance for yourself.

That's right. If you want to cut your taxes, the ideas are going to have to come from you. You should read and listen. Learn the latest techniques and seize upon them. Then, you can go to your lawyer or accountant with information to apply to your situation.

Fortunately, there are hundreds of tax cutting techniques around. Taken together, *they have the potential to save you a bundle.*

Did you know . . .

- that a corporation can invest in stocks and pay a maximum tax of only 6.9% on dividend income?
- that a loss of a tree in a storm can be tax deductible as a casualty loss?
- that the expense of looking for a new job—

including travel, meals, copying your resume—is tax deductible, even if you decide to stay with your present job?

• that under some circumstances you can deduct entertainment expense even when business is not discussed?

• that the cost of your home security system is partly tax deductible if used to protect investment items?

• that your payments to an ex-wife may or may not be tax deductible depending on how you word your settlement?

• that the cost of studying for an MBA or other advanced degree can be deductible even if you don't hold a job while you are in school?

• there are seven states that levy no state taxes (income)?

• that the new law permits you to write off $5,000 in new equipment immediately?

• that it sometimes makes good sense, taxwise, to turn down an inheritance?

• that the annual interest statements sent out by mortgage companies are often wrong? (Check yours carefully.)

It's A Family Affair

The real opportunities for cutting taxes occur when you plan well in advance instead of waiting until April.

The taxpayer with high earnings, a spouse and children has outstanding opportunities to slash taxes. If you own your own business or have substantial assets, the opportunities multiply.

A favorite technique is called "income splitting." The idea is to take the income of one person who is in, let's say, the 50% bracket, and spread it around among other family members who are in much lower brackets.

Remember, if you are in the 50% bracket, you have to earn $2 if you want one dollar left to spend on your children. That's why it's so wonderful to learn strategies like these:

• A doctor transferred his medical equipment and furnishings to a trust for the benefit of his children, the trust to last for ten years. He then leased the equipment from the trust, thus switching income to his children, whose income is so low they pay virtually no tax at all.

• Instead of saving money to put his son through college, one man loaned his son $50,000, interest free, the note payable in full at the end of 7 years, when his son will have finished college. The $50,000 is now in a money fund where it's generating $6,000 income per year—taxed at the son's 16% rate instead of the father's 50% rate. When the son finishes school, the father can request repayment of the entire loan.

• A husband and wife with a small business employ each of their three children. The kids earn $5,300 per year tax free. (Each child gets $2,300 tax free on their own return, plus an additional $1,000 exemption; and each has an individual IRA account.) Meanwhile, the husband and wife still get to claim an exemption for each child on their joint return.

There are literally dozens of strategies like these for keeping your income out of Uncle Sam's pocket. I can't begin to describe them all, but here's one more.

For example, if your wife isn't working now and you file a joint return, you should encourage her to get a part-time job or at-home business that will pay at least $2,000 per year. She can open her own IRA, and the whole $2,000 will be untaxed. Not bad, for a middle income taxpayer.

The Best Single Technique for Reducing Your Taxes

The most outstanding tax strategy is simple, legal and available to anyone who has some savings. You don't have to itemize to take advantage of it. And it will actually reduce your chances of an audit. Yet even the most sophisticated taxpayers often neglect this technique, even as they go out on a limb with exotic deductions.

The strategy I'm talking about is to switch your ordinary income into long-term capital gains, whenever possible.

Long-term capital gains are now taxed at a maximum rate of 20% but that's for taxpayers in the 50% tax bracket on their ordinary income. For those in lower brackets, the capital gains rate can amount to practically nothing. In any case, you don't pay a cent in taxes until you sell the investment, which may be years in the future.

Just a word of warning against the obsession with

high yield money funds and other forms of current income. Unless you must have the income now, consider growth stocks, gold, real estate and other investments that allow you to defer taxes until future years.

A Word About Tax Shelters

What is a tax shelter? Some people use the word loosely to mean any method that saves you taxes. To a tax professional, however, "tax shelter" means an investment that gives you huge deductions against your current income, while any profit from the shelter is deferred well into the future. Usually, the risks are very great. But the rewards can be very high if you choose the investment wisely.

The problem is, the tax shelter market is flooded with risky, dubious and downright illegal schemes. That is a shame, because it makes it hard to find the shelters that are good investments in addition to being unbeatable ways to cut your taxes. Fortunately, there's good news! The new tax law throws cold water on a lot of the craziest schemes. At the same time, it makes sound tax shelter investments more attractive than ever.

Here are some tax slashing tips to consider:

- Timber deals: little-known, but safe and profitable.
- Spreading your risks among several shelters.
- Run, don't walk, in the opposite direction when invited to invest in a Broadway play.
- Which type of shelter was the big winner in the new tax law?
- Big write-offs (and little-known dangers) from equipment leasing ventures.

Plan Ahead to Minimize Your IRS Bill

In 1925 average Americans worked more than a full day in every week to support their government. It already costs more than their pleasure and almost as much as their vice. It was predicted that in another century, it will begin to cost as much as their necessities. That point has now been reached!

Average Americans now labor a bit more than five months a year to pay their federal, state, and local taxes. In spite of periodic pronouncement by the Great Communicator, the situation worsens month by month. Despite the much-heralded Reagan tax cuts, the net effect of the federal government taxing policy has been much different than the president would have us believe. The same month that the first installment of the biggest tax cut in American history went into effect, Social Security taxes were boosted. Thus, on the pay stubs of those with incomes of less than $40,000 a year, there were hardly any benefits from the new tax schedules. And when the effects of bracket creep (the extra taxes one pays because inflation has kicked them into a higher bracket) are considered as well, it turns out that many low-to-moderate-income people ended up paying more after the cut than they had a year earlier.

While rates of federal taxation have been rising, those mandated by the states have been taking an even more predatory turn. On average, every man, woman and child in the country now pays upwards of $600 a year to state government. This is more than double the comparable figure for a decade ago. And the jump in state taxation since the beginning of 1980 indicates worse things to come.

Although the contention that more taxes are related to specific needs of society sounds plausible, an examination of taxing policies past and present suggests that such increases do not in fact mirror real needs. Another force in driving them skyward.

The point, of course, is that the specific reasons given at any particular time for increased government spending and taxation are largely irrelevant. What really matters is that once government has reached a certain size and has the power, the physical mechanisms and the assent (sullen or otherwise) to coopt an ever-greater share of a country's wealth, it invariably does so. Almost any pretext will suffice to justify exorbitant taxation once those conditions are met. In Italy, which is in some ways the most civilized country in the Western World, the official tax rate is treated as taxable income.

It is very difficult to construct or justify tax defenses at the end of the year. The best time to do that is from the year's start. With that in mind, here are some basic tips on how to keep most of what you earn. (For specific problems you should, of course, consult your own tax advisor).

Tips On Keeping Your Earnings

Get in the habit of keeping complete records of all income and expenditures. A daily log of business travel, for example, is an excellent record to have in case one's travel is questioned during an audit. The same type of records should be kept for business related entertainment, purchase of work clothes, charitable deductions, etc. Granted, this bookkeeping is tedious, but it is much simpler to have this data on hand at tax time than to try to construct it from memory. Receipts also hold up better than total recall during an audit.

Consider the "tax factor" in all new earnings and investments. Make more in ways that are taxed less if you have any control over the form your compensation takes. When looking at a prospective investment, figure it after tax return, not its pretax return. Consider not only the after-tax return for the present year, but also how it will affect your net income situation in future years, when your salary may be different.

Understand the different types of shelters available to lessen your tax obligation. Some, like a house or an IRA, are very secure and almost a necessity for people who are above a certain income level—say, $30,000 for a couple. Other shelters, however, have inherent drawbacks, either because of their risky natures or because a person has to tie up capital for many years, often without the right to tap it even in emergencies.

Dispel the notion that there is something immoral or illegal about taking adequate steps to protect yourself from paying "your share" of the country's tax burden. "By means which the law provides," reads the United States Supreme Court ruling, "a taxpayer has the right to decrease the amount of what otherwise would be his/her taxes, or altogether avoid them."

What Is To Be Done?

Although American history is instructive, and though

precedents set by other lands suggest eventual remedies to our present tax dilemma, people have to live in the here and now. They make attempts to alleviate their own tax burdens. The most valuable of these measures begins with a simple perception of just how vital adequate tax planning is today. Anyone who thinks in terms of "how much I make" instead of "how much I keep" is living in goo-goo land. The prime aim of one's future economic activities must give absolute priority to increasing after-tax wealth, not boosting paper income.

That has been the approach of Europeans for many years, and it is the basis of a revolution that is now taking place in the compensation and benefit programs of some of this country's most progressive corporations. Their remuneration packages are coming to consist not only of cash, but also company cars, extra vacation time, generous moving expenses, access to company financial planning services and other similar benefits. The smart employer is learning to pay non-taxable coin, and the smart employee in a position to demand a better deal, is learning to look toward the after-tax implications of his/her raises.

The same principle can often be applied when one works for a smaller company. The thing to remember is that the same outlay for an employer can be applied toward many forms of compensation. Fifty dollars more a week in salary is the same to a company as a $50 car rental for an employee who has a genuine business related need for a car. The $2,600 a year in free transportation the employee gets, however, is not taxable to the employee.

Earlier I discussed dividing income among family members—here is how it can reduce the tax at various income levels.

Taxable Income	Tax Bill (income not divided)	Family Tax Bill (income divided in 2)	Family Tax Bill (income divided in 3)	Family Tax Bill (income divided in 4)
$100,000	$34,190	$26,752	$21,418	$18,247
75,000	22,614	16,742	13,418	11,426
50,000	12,014	8,589	6,967	5,991
25,000	3,760	2,831	2,296	1,915

In conclusion—become something other than a wage earner. Taxpayers who have their income from wages pay the highest percentage of income to the United States Treasury, are stuck with the narrowest range of deductions and generally do the least about it. When Congress raises taxes, as it seems to do yearly, Schedule A on your form 1040 is hit the hardest.

One way out—adopt a business strategy—make your hobby into a business. Start a part-time family business—become an independent contractor. Did you know the I.R.S. discriminates in favor of a business, especially incorporated business?

With your own business, your list of possible deductions goes from about 6% to an almost unlimited amount—to the extent that you can legitimately create an overlap between your personal and business expenses. In essence then, you can make the IRS partially pay the bills!

Fueling Anxiety

The IRS push to enforce the negligence penalty is so new that many tax professionals still haven't felt the shove. But loud protests from accounts in the East and Midwest—apparently among the first to be penalized—leave little doubt that the IRS has embarked on a campaign to fine them for a host of technical errors. Most accountants suspect the IRS of a hidden motive. Besides using the negligence penalty as Congress intended—to weed out incompetent or dishonest preparers—they think the IRS wants to frighten them into "red flagging" each questionable item on a return, a weapon IRS Commissioner Jerome Kurtz wanted written into law as early as 1977.

The IRS had fueled accountants' anxiety by refusing to discuss details of its new policy. IRS spokespeople claim, "Everyone wants us to say publicly what we're doing, but we won't. If tax preparers feel insecure about those penalties, then I'd say they're right to be overly defensive." In private some officials concede that the new enforcement program is intended in part to intimidate tax professionals into cooperating more fully with the government.

Untimely Hacking

People who stand to lose the most from the new IRS policy are those who claim lots of deductions: business expenses of the "three-martini-lunch" kind, unusually large charitable donations, and accelerated depreciation on investment property, to name a few. But any taxpayer with moderately complex finances also may lose. Accountants will be less inclined to give clients the benefits of the doubt whenever the law can be read two ways or evidence for a deduction is less than airtight.

The IRS has not chosen the best of times to hack away at the relationship between accountants and taxpayer. New complications in the tax code make the service of a good accountant a necessity for most people with moderately large income. It's probably a good idea to quiz your accountant about the new negligence penalty and, if he/she seems overly intimidated by it, to consider changing accountants.

Those who do their own tax returns, and 60% do, have one big advantage over commercial tax preparers. If an ordinary taxpayer makes an honest mistake on his/her taxes, the most it is likely to cost is a 12% late payment fee on the amount of tax still owed—and that fee is deductible. The prize for the most bamboozling addition to the tax code probably should go to the new "alternative minimum tax," which affects people with extra large deductions or capital gains. Investors with sizable gains, for example, have to calculate their tax two ways and pay the higher of the two results. Anyone faced with this new tax has little choice but to consult a pro.

Whose Side Is the Tax Preparer On?

For those who traditionally file tax returns with the aid of a professional service, there is another whole area to be considered. Tax preparers are under a new threat of penalties for helping you pay less.

Here's how to keep yours from defecting.

The millions of taxpayers who will rely on commercial tax preparers are apt to find them acting less like comrades-in-arms and more like Internal Revenue Service agents in disguise. The reason: in the past year or so the government has begun pressuring accountants to treat clients much as an IRS auditor would. Under negligence-penalty provisions enacted by Congress in 1976 but not enforced until recently, accountants say the IRS has been harassing them with fines of $100 per return for not catching petty errors that result in lower taxes—even when the client is to blame.

This is changing the light in which tax preparers are viewing taxpayers and in which taxpayers may have to view preparers. While the change in relationships may not be dramatic enough to make you forgo an accountant's services, you may well have to prepare your records far more diligently than ever before. Those whose taxes aren't too complicated may find it advantageous to do without a tax preparer. Unfortunately, tax forms haven't become any simpler. Whether or not you've done your own taxes previously, you'll need to know about some new wrinkles described later in this article.

More For Less

Many accountants will now ask for extra documentation from clients, others may insist on reviewing client's income and deduction records. Here and there, tax preparers are asking clients to sign statements to the effect that the information the client provides is completely accurate.

Inevitably, tax preparers' self-defense measures will be reflected in their fees. "If I have to spend extra time auditing a client, a return that would have cost $100 is going to cost probably $140." Another accountant has boosted his average fee 5% to establish a "reserve fund" for penalties. While paying more, taxpayers may be getting less help. "When it comes to a gray area in the law, most tax preparers are going to look out for themselves rather than the taxpayer."

Many accountants, particularly those in larger, better-known firms, vow to resist the penalties. They would rather spend thousands of dollars fighting the IRS in court than agree to a single $100 fine that casts doubt on their professionalism. In their view the government is using the negligence penalty to break up their traditional alliance with the taxpayer. We're supposed to be the taxpayer's advocate, not their inquisitor.

Counting Trips

The IRS short form 1040A is still comparatively uncomplicated, but a great many people cannot use it—single people who made over $20,000 last year; married couples filing jointly who made over $40,000 or anybody who wants to itemize deductions or has significant investment income. People in those categories had better start gathering their cancelled checks, credit card statements and receipts.

Whether you hire a preparer or not, detailed records

will come in handy. Each check to a doctor, dentist or optician, for instance, probably represents at least one trip to the office. It is thus a reminder of one of the tax breaks most commonly overlooked, medical deductions for transportation costs. In some cases the transportation costs may push total medical expenses over 3% of your adjusted gross income, the point at which they become deductible.

It's best to organize your documents according to the major sections of the tax return. First, collect documents pertaining to income: W-2 salary statements, 1099 forms reporting savings accounts and investment income, brokerage stubs, mutual fund statements establishing the amounts of investment gains and losses, and miscellaneous income such as alimony, tax refunds and gambling gains. Next, list such deductibles as state and local taxes, charitable contributions, health insurance payments, medical and dental costs not reimbursed by insurance, and interest payments on mortages, car and other installment loans and credit card accounts. Don't forget to deduct the cost of professional dues, equipment, books or periodicals that pertain to your business or investments, and last year's bill from your tax preparer.

Be Aware of Changes

Be on the lookout for the latest changes which constantly occur.

Deductible car mileage. The standard mileage deduction for business use of a car has been raised from

18½¢ to 20¢ a mile for the first 15,000 miles. Thereafter, the rate goes from 10¢ to 11¢ a mile. The use of a car on charitable missions, for trips to doctors, or for job related moving purposes has been raised to 9¢ a mile.

Unemployment benefits. There's less charitable news for people who were unemployed. Unemployment used to be tax free, but as of 1979, you must pay taxes on half of any jobless benefits that put your total income over $20,000 if you are single, or $25,000 if you are married and filing jointly.

Tax Credits. Dollar for dollar, tax credits are better than tax deductions because they are subtracted from the amount of income on which you pay taxes. The tax credit for political contributions has been doubled to a maximum $50 for a single person or $100 for a couple. You can claim credit for only half the money you donated. To get the full $50 credit, you had to donate at least $100 to a political party or candidate. Unfortunately for tax revolutionaries, opponents of nuclear power and crusaders for other causes, the tax credit can't be used for contributions to any political campaign other than one intended to help a candidate get elected. Neither can you claim as a credit the actual cost of food or entertainment included in tickets to political fund-raising dinners and similar events.

You may qualify for two kinds of residential energy credits. Investments in an active or passive solar energy equipment or in wind or geothermal gear gives you a credit equal to 30% of the first $2,000 spent and 20% of the next $8,000, for a maximum credit of $2,200.

There is also a credit of 15% of the first $2,000 spent for insulation or other fuel conservation equipment in a home built before April 20, 1977.

You can count toward this credit more efficient furnace controls or burners, new storm windows and doors, automatic thermostats, and exterior caulking and weather stripping. If you've spent less than $10 on energy saving materials, you can combine unclaimed credits from year to year and claim them anytime through 1985.

Windfall for Heirs

People who employed others may benefit from two changes in tax credits. If you hired a welfare recipient or a former welfare recipient now enrolled in the government's work incentive program, you can claim a 35% credit on the first $6,000 of wages. You are allowed to claim the child care credit if you paid your child's grandparents to babysit so that you could go to work. The credit—20% of costs with a maximum credit of $400 for one child and $800 for two or more children—previously applied to other relatives. But you can't claim the child care credit if you also claim the babysitter as a dependent.

Keeping a friend

As this and other new bits of tax arcana suggest, there's all the more reason to hope accountants and other tax preparers can resist the IRS pressure to deputize them. They have all they can do as it is to follow the windings and rewindings of the United States tax code. Since ordinary taxpayers cannot hope to master the code, simple justice dictates that they be allowed to keep at least one friend at court.

"The only difference between stumbling blocks and stepping stones is the way we use them."

—Anonymous

"Everytime a person puts a new idea across, they find ten people have thought of it before them—but they only thought of it."

—Henry G. Weaver

DALE O. FERRIER

Dale O. Ferrier Associates
P.O. Box 10539
Fort Wayne, IN 46852
(219) 744-4373 ● (219) 749-8925

Dale O. Ferrier

Throughout his career, Dr. Dale O. Ferrier has been an entrepreneur involved in several management and professional ventures, concurrent with his management of the family-owned business, Indiana Wire Die Company, which he now serves as president.

Dale's speeches and cassette album are liberally laced with humor and motivational and inspirational themes. He leads management seminars for all-size groups on topics geared to the small businessman.

He has been a member of the National Speakers Association for nearly four years, and holds a certificate of professionalism in that association.

Dale is also a published writer, having appeared in The Rotarian, The Toastmaster *and numerous other publications. He is a graduate of Fort Wayne Bible College, holds a Masters Degree in Business from Indiana University, and has a Ph.D. from Walden University.*

He is listed in Who's Who in the Midwest, International Who's Who of Intellectuals *and the* International Book of Honor.

MOTIVATION IS SPELLED WITH FOUR C's
by Dale O. Ferrier

"One never mounts so high as when one does not know how high he is going."

—Napoleon I

The old man's life had ticked down to the last remaining days when the word came. His son, president of the corporation into which the old man had poured most of his seventy-five years, had disappeared in a private plane over a remote part of Brazil. When someone finally was able to combine the courage and the tact to tell him, the reaction was as they all expected: fear, sorrow, anger and despair. Then the miracle happened. Instead of dying as he should have done, the old man rallied and within the hour was on the telephone directing the search for his son. The next morning, resisting all well-meaning restraints, he was up earlier than almost anyone else and made clear he was going to the plant. They needed leadership and he was their leader.

By the time the son was found ten days later the old man appeared ten years younger and was firmly in control of the family's vast enterprises. He continued in that role while the younger man recuperated from some moderately severe injuries. Later, instead of returning to his bed to die, the old man, an important part of the leadership team again, continued to direct the affairs of the organization in a manner reminiscent of decades earlier.

Miracle of Motivation

How could such a thing be? Well, it happened because the old man wasn't suffering from a terminal illness at all. He was suffering from terminal *boredom*. The miracle wasn't a miracle of medicine. It was a *miracle of motivation*. As soon as he realized that he was needed, he struggled into the old armor and began to act like the old warrior; and as he did, the miracle took place. As he tasted, gingerly at first, the old flavors of success and realized that he was still the man he used to be, even if the container was a bit knocked about, the juices began to flow. It wasn't long after he realized he was needed that his old powers were restored. The motivation was the miracle, but success was the catalyst.

Success and motivation are a peculiar set of twins; somewhat like the Brothers Karimotsov. Each is so dependent on the other that together they make a reinforcing cycle. Only the motivated are very successful, and only those who meet with some measure of success stay motivated very long. Therefore, it is important that we know how to attain success if our motivation is going to have more substance than a mere raising of momentary goose bumps.

Dictionary Definition of Success

Thinking about success and what it really means prompted me to get my *Funk & Wagnalls Standard Dictionary* down from the bookshelf behind my desk. Funk said that a success is "one embarked on a favorable or prosperous course." Wagnall chimed in with "one who has satisfactorily completed an intended objective." Their definition seemed all right as far as it went but the more I thought about it, the more I was sure a success far surpasses the scope of formal definition. So, I added a supplemental definition of my own.

Ferrier's Supplemental Definition of Success

A "Success" is one who:
1. Pursues excellence and is not satisfied with less.
2. Refuses to complain about bad breaks and blame them for poor performance.
3. Is more interested in the team's success than in personal glory.
4. Gives his or her best every time, all the time, in spite of how they feel, not because of it.
5. Is pleased with no less than a job well done, even if no one else is aware of it.
6. Desires and stimulates growth—personally as well as in those over whom he or she has influence.

7. Never quits, even when quitting is the most attractive alternative!

Four C's of Success

As in almost every activity involving some degree of skill, the basics are most important. In the efforts to be successful, I believe there are four elements that are vital. They are basic and almost simplistic, but for that I don't apologize. I remember over a decade ago when an almost unknown football coach came from out of nowhere and took over a third-rate football team of has-beens and never-weres. By drilling, unrelentingly, into their bodies and minds the consistent execution of the basics, and into their spirits the attitudes of winners, he turned them into the World-Champion Green Bay Packers. The coaching philosophy of Vince Lombardi was, "The team which most consistently executes the basics is the team that will most consistently win." Therefore, if we are going to be truly successful— consistently successful, then we too, must consistently execute well the basics necessary for success.

Competence

The first basic for consistent success is competence. We must be able to do something very well. To be successful is to be able to achieve worthwhile goals and that requires a very special combination. Achievement is the blending of generous amounts of knowledge, skill, positive attitude and consistent performance.

Knowledge. The world's store of knowledge is growing at an ever-increasing rate of speed. This is partly due to the fact that more people are working to find out more things than ever before, and partly because they have better means of learning than they ever had in the past.

In chemistry, for example, we have discovered new elements that, a generation ago, nobody knew existed. In astronomy and planetary science we are discovering new bodies in the heavens every year. We have had eye-witness reports of what the moon is like and even watched as our own people explored its surface.

We can store more in a tray of modern microfilm than the entire array of knowledge that was accumulated in the great library of Alexandria and scan it all at breath-taking speed. It has been estimated that in the space of a single generation, the world will have four times as much knowledge as it has today; and more than ninety percent of what will be known fifty years from now is unknown today!

In the 1940's the early mainframe computers required their own rooms, needed buildings full of electronics, cost over a million dollars each, required huge teams of highly trained support personnel, weighed over 60,000 pounds, contained over 18,000 tubes, but processed large quantities of material in seconds. These early monsters are now put to shame by children's video games and pocket calculators. Today's computers no longer work in seconds, they work in pico-seconds. A pico-second is to a second as a second is to 30,000 years.

The current capabilities of third-generation computers is mind boggling. Yet, even before we can catch our breath, along comes word that a Rockville, Maryland, company, EMV Associates, believes it can have a biochip in production by the early 1990's. If they are right, the biochip will obsolete the 65K chip that is the basis of the unbelievable performances we are hearing about today. These biochips will be made from protein and will be triggered by enzymes rather than electricity. The units, called Moletons, will perform at the molecular level rather than the gross level of molecular masses. Because they work biochemically and are based on enzyme action rather than electricity, they will eliminate the pesky heat dissipation problems of today's powerful computers. Talk about micro-minaturization, biochips may be only .01 micron across. Therefore, 6,200 of them would only be as long as the average human hair is wide. With biochips, 64 trillion bits of information could be put into the space of one of today's 64K memory chips!

James McAlear, EMV's president says: "At these circuit densities, all data stored in the world's computers today could be stored in a single biochip computer." The biochips of the 1990's will make the 64K chip seem like a lumbering dinosaur; for not only will they be one billion times more powerful, but they will be 100 million times quicker. Joseph Moskal of the National Institute of Health says devices made from these heat-free, super-fast, and mega-powerful biochips could be used to restore lost physical functions—even eyesight.

Power of Knowledge

There is no doubt, knowledge is an extremely important ingredient in the success formula today. Some have even said "Knowledge *is* power!"; however, this is just not true. For, if knowledge were power, the most powerful people in the world would be librarians because they are the custodians of knowledge. It is not knowledge that is power. It is the *application* of knowledge that is power. It is important, of course, how much you know. But, it is vastly more important how effectively you can apply that knowledge. If I ever find it necessary to have major surgery of any kind, I want the surgeon who has completed the most successful operations working on me; not the one who has read the most books about it and has scored the highest on the examinations.

Skill. With knowledge we must couple skill; and skill only comes with practice. You were probably told by a coach or a piano teacher about the importance of practice. You may even have heard the old saying, "Practice makes perfect." Unfortunately, this is one old saying that is not *quite* true. Practice does *not* make perfect; it only makes permanent. Only the practice of perfection makes perfect. Therefore, while practice is important, it needs to be done under the supervision of a competent teacher and guide. The poet's observation, "No man is an island, but each is a part of the main ...," is certainly true when it comes to the development of skill. No one is truly independent. We must each depend upon someone to help us achieve our highest potential.

Attitude. Psychologists and educators have replicated many studies that show a direct correlation between attitude and achievement. In the sports world, the player with mediocre ability and an outstanding attitude who gives championship performances has become a cliche. Likewise in business, there are many

It is impossible to do anything that is inconsistent with our own self-image. In other words, if we don't really believe we can succeed, it is sure that we won't. This doesn't preclude our taking risks, but it does preclude our achieving anything that we cannot see ourselves doing. As soon as we conceive in our minds something is impossible, it is. The great Scandinavian runner Nurmi was asked back in 1938 if anyone would ever be able to run the mile in four minutes. He replied: "The four-minute barrier will be broken when someone thinks he can do it. The barrier exists in the mind, not in the legs." Twenty years later, Roger Bannister ran a mile in less than four minutes for the first time. Today, it isn't much of a track meet if someone doesn't run the mile in less than four minutes. It is strictly a matter of confidence.

However, we must be careful not to mistake arrogance for confidence. Those individuals who boast and bluster and seem so superconfident are in fact, the psychologists tell us, often covering up a deep feeling of inadequacy. Rather than being the confident persons they would like us to believe they are, they are insecure, unsure and frightened of the future. Real confidence is usually displayed in a wrapping of serenity and quiet thoughtfulness. The confident person has not always succeeded in the conventional sense; but he or she has plumbed the depths of his abilities, has accepted himself and his limitations, and faces the future expecting to grow and accomplish even greater things. He does not commit himself to the foolhardy; but when he does engage in the battle, it is with an expectation that when the dust settles and the results are in, he will be victorious. To be truly successful, we need to cultivate that kind of self-image and that kind of attitude.

One very good way of cultivating a healthy and realistic opinion of ourselves and our abilities is honest self-evaluation. While it would be foolish to ignore our limitations, it would be even more foolish to dwell on them. To really appreciate what a marvelous piece of God's handiwork we are, we should concentrate on our strengths.

I have found it helpful periodically to take an inventory of strengths. Occasionally, when I am not facing some great challenge or threatening set of circumstances which might distort the evaluation, it is helpful to sit and consider successes of the past. Let me suggest that you take paper and pencil, find a quiet place, an uninterrupted bit of time, and do your own strengths inventory. Think back over your past, and write down those things you can remember as positive accomplishments. Don't try to be modest at this point, and don't try to be grandiose. If you feel good about it, no matter how insignificant it may seem, write it down. Also, don't keep discarding positive things you remember just because it was a team effort, and you weren't the star of the team. If it was possible, if you succeeded, write it down.

After you have listed as many as you can remember, beside or beneath each one write down the strengths or personal characteristics you think helped you to be successful. Continue this exercise until you have created your own comprehensive inventory of success. It will be useful for several purposes—to help you get a more objective, positive picture of yourself as a worthwhile human being with great potential and a good track record, and also it will be useful in the future when you experience a temporary setback, and you need to pull up your socks and get back in the battle. A review of your success inventory will help you recharge your confidence batteries and get back to it. Or someday, when a great but challenging, perhaps even overwhelming, opportunity is before you, and you aren't sure you can handle it; a thorough review of your success inventory may give you that little extra confidence you need to move ahead again with the boldness of championship performance.

Confidence is definitely a keystone of success, and we will never be all that God intends us to be without it.

Communication

The third "C" of success is communication. Communication, in its essence, is simply the creation of a picture in the mind of someone else. Hopefully, if you are skilled at communicating, the idea received by the other person is the one you intended it to be. Be that as it may, we do communicate, whether intentionally or unconsciously, all the time. The ability to influence the pictures in other people's minds is a gift given by God only to the crowning glory of His creation. Only human beings communicate ideas, and it is a precious gift too often wasted or abused.

To be as successful as it is possible for us to be, we must be skillful communicators. How do we communicate? We communicate by:

What We Say! The words we speak are the most obvious means of our communication. They are the containers of our meaning. They are affected by many other things, but they basically transport our thoughts from one mind to another. Each word is like a little railroad car that is loaded full of meaning and then connected with a lot of other little cars of meaning. These cars then become trains of thought we send on their way. We hope they arrive just as we sent them; but unfortunately, things happen to them along the way. They are held up, hijacked if you will, and by the time they get to their destination, the meaning has changed so dramatically that we would hardly recognize it if we could inspect it at "receiving." Like Jesse James' gang of old, attitude, emotion, misunderstanding, experience, idiom, perspective and a host of other gang members lie in wait for our innocent, unsuspecting little train of thought and fall upon it in ruthless malevolence and maliciously vandalize the cargo. It is a wonder sometimes that anyone ever comes close to being understood!

The Way We Say It! While words are the basics of communications, they have a huge supporting cast. In addition to what we say, our gestures, eye contact, body language, vocal tonations and inflections, clothing and every sensual stimulation communicate our message to others. It may not be what we think it is, and most likely is not; but it is communicating—either to support or deny the cargo that our words are carrying. To be more conscious of this second dimension of communication is to be a more skillful communicator.

Conscience

Finally, we come to that ingredient of success which, more than all the others, sets off the truly successful from those who are deceived by a few temporary baubles or "huzzas" into thinking that they are something special. To be able to sleep the sleep of the just, to look with innocent eyes into the faces of friends, and to be at peace with God and man—that is true success. The bedrock of this kind of success is called honor by some, a clear conscience by others, and by many—integrity. Whatever it is, it is something special; and we all know it when we see it.

Shakespeare put it best when he said: ". . . This above all. To thine own self be true, and it must follow as the night the day, thou canst not then be false to any man."

I had the privilege a few years ago to see this kind of integrity in action, and it was a true serendipity. I was playing in a handball tournament at Indianapolis; and while waiting to play in the quarter finals of the Novice Class, I went down to the glass court to watch the "A" players in their semi-finals. A Hawaiian student from Indiana University was playing a tall, thin doctor from Indianapolis. The winner of the match was going to go up against Ray Elliot, the reigning Indiana State Handball Champion; there was a lot at stake, and it was a hard-fought match.

As if to verify that old saw, "Truth is often stranger than fiction," the match went down to a score of 20 to 20 in the final game. The young Hawaiian served a nice lob into the left rear corner. The doctor had a hard time returning it; and it ricocheted off his hand into the far corner, close to the floor. It looked like one of those lucky returns that are impossible for the opponent to reach; but the student dove for the ball, and those of us in the balcony saw the ball shoot like a bullet into the crotch of the corner and just trickle out across the floor. The referee pronounced, "Point! Game! Match!"; and as far as we were concerned the student had won and would be playing in the finals that afternoon.

As we were turning to go down to the door of the court to congratulate the young man on a fine performance, we heard him call out: "Hold it, Ref! That was a wrist ball." A wrist ball is one that strikes the wrist or arm above the glove and is illegal in the game of handball. The Hawaiian student had lost the serve instead of winning the game. The score was still 20 to 20 and the doctor served a freakish serve that hugged the wall, and when it hit the floor took a crazy bounce and was not returnable. This time when the referee said, "Point! Game! Match!" it was for the doctor, and it was final.

When I got down from the balcony, I noticed that there were more people gathered around the Hawaiian student congratulating him than were gathered around the winner. I believe the reason for their display of approval was simply that they realized they had seen a demonstration of real integrity. Most of us there were handball players, and we knew that no one in the world knew that the ball had struck the student's arm instead of his hand. We knew that the easiest thing in the world would have been for him to just keep quiet and accept the match. However, his integrity was worth far more than the fleeting glory of a handball tournament win; and he obviously did what was right because it was the right thing to do.

Who was the real "success" when that game was over? Of course, the doctor was successful as far as the score was concerned, but the student was successful in even more important ways. He had, unwittingly and maybe even unwillingly, become an example of integrity for us all. Remember, you, too, are an example to someone; unwittingly and perhaps even unwillingly, but an example all the same. What kind of example are you?

Look Up

As the days get shorter and the nights colder, you may find yourself looking up in response to the thunder of wings above. As you look skyward you are likely to see the telltale V of Canadian geese heading south. When you see them, think of why they are flying in that formation. Naturalists tell us that as the geese fly in V formation, each bird provides a lift from his wings for his wingmate. As they take turns flying at the point of the V, each one takes his turn at breaking the wind and taking the buffeting that goes with his term of leadership. This kind of configuration allows the birds to fly some 70 percent further than any one bird could fly alone.

Like those geese we, too provide lift for some others; and if in the process we take a little beating and buffeting, it is our integrity that keeps us at the point and sees us through the storms.

Conclusion

Therefore, as we go through life, we will experience the motivation of success if we just spell it with the four "C"s:

> COMPETENCE,
> CONFIDENCE,
> CONSCIENCE and
> COMMUNICATION.

SUCCESS SEMINAR SERIES
ANTHOLOGIES

#1: SUCCESS SECRETS! How 18 everyday women became builders and famous speakers! Role models! Beautiful hardback. Stimulating, inspirational, how to build your business and your life. ■ **$11.95**

#2: POSITIVE POWER PEOPLE. Men and women of achievement radiate positive attitudes, inspire readers to greater success. Foreword Cavett Robert. Book, hardback. ■ **$12.95**

#3. THE PEARL OF POTENTIALITY. Are you ready to catch it? An anthology of women of achievement from a woman. Train engineer to inventors, to speakers a wealth of inspiration! Hardback, beautiful gift for women beginning their careers. ■ **$11.95**

 # 4: HERE IS GENIUS. Men and women tell the stories of achievement and inspiration by opening the *genius channel*. Foreword by Dr. Norman Vincent Peale. Book, hardback. ■ **$11.95**

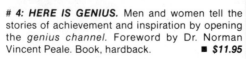

 # 5: THOSE MARVELOUS MENTORS. Amazing stories of the influences on their lives of top notch speakers and business people. Hardback. Foreword by former Arizona Congressman Somers White. Outstanding! ■ *$13.95*

#6: STAR SPANGLED SPEAKERS. Here are stories of the Space Shuttle, the Statue of Liberty, Americans who have overcome. Hardback. True stories of the people who won the battles of life. ■ *$13.95*

 # 7: THE SUNSHINERS. Secrets of humorous speakers. You'll laugh, you'll learn, you'll love them. Hardback. The speakers who light up your life. ■ *$13.95*

 # 8: THE GREAT PERSUADERS. Sales and sales management. The top managers in the United States give you their best information. Hardback. A treasure trove of how-to and when-to by the very top people. ■ *$16.95*

 # 9: *HOW TO ENTER THE WORLD OF PAID SPEAKING* by *DOTTIE WALTERS*, C.S.P. Full four-hour cassette album. Rally speaker tells you how to start, what to charge, and how to find paying customers. Rated TOPS by Cavett Robert. How to begin where you are, how to ask for the right fee. How to sell products from the platform, how to promote yourself at no cost. How to locate those paying audiences. What to do if they have no money—to make more than ever.

■ *4-hour album $59.00*

 # 10: *NEVER UNDERESTIMATE THE SELLING POWER OF A WOMAN* by *DOTTIE WALTERS*, C.S.P. The FAMOUS bestseller. The best sales book ever written by a woman for women in sales. Used as a textbook by many national sales firms. Easy to read, full of power. The classic! Hardback, book.

■ *$13.95*

 # 11: SELLING POWER OF A WOMAN by DOTTIE WALTERS, C.S.P. Big six-hour cassette album, full course, six cassettes. Dynamite! This is IT! Top course sales! ■ *Cassette album, $69.00*

 # 12: SEVEN SECRETS OF SELLING TO WOMEN by DOTTIE WALTERS, C.S.P. One hour cassette. After listening to this cassette, you can sell ANY woman ANYTHING! . . . so they say! Amazing! ■ *Cassette, single, $9.95*

SHARING IDEAS
Newsletter for Speakers
includes list of 150 booking agents

■ *$35.00 1 year, $60.00 2 years*
Sample copy, $3.00

(Foreign countries add $10 annual postage)

SEE ORDER FORM NEXT PAGE

ORDER FORM

BOOKS

No.	Quantity	Amt.	No.	Quantity	Amt.	No.	Quantity	Amt.

NEWSLETTERS

Check Enclosed
Master Charge _____
Bankam./icard
VISA
Acct. No. _____

Expiration Date _____

Ship To:

Name _____

Address _____

City _____ State _____ Zip _____

Signature _____

Add 6% Sales Tax in Calif.
Plus $1.00 Shipping and handling per item.
$2.00 out of the U.S.A.
American Currency only.
$20.00 Min. on charge card orders (M.C. or VISA)

Total _____

Royal Cassettes*Books*Speeches, Inc 600 W. Foothill Blvd., Glendora, CA 91740

ORDER FORM

BOOKS

No.	Quantity	Amt.	No.	Quantity	Amt.	No.	Quantity	Amt.

NEWSLETTERS

Check Enclosed
Master Charge _____
Bankamericard
VISA
Acct. No. _____

Expiration Date _____

Ship To:

Name _____

Address _____

City _____ State _____ Zip _____

Signature _____

Total _____

Add 6% Sales Tax in Calif.
Plus $1.00 Shipping and handling per item.
$2.00 out of the U.S.A.
American Currency only.
$20.00 Min. on charge card orders (M.C. or VISA)

Royal Cassettes*Books*Speeches, Inc 600 W. Foothill Blvd., Glendora, CA 91740